MAKING
MATH Accessible
to Students with SPECIAL NEEDS

Practical Tips and Suggestions

Grades
3–5

Solution Tree | Press

r4
Educated Solutions

Visit **go.solution-tree.com/specialneeds** to download reproducibles and other materials associated with this book.

Published by Solution Tree Press

555 North Morton Street
Bloomington, IN 47404
800.733.6786 (toll free) / 812.336.7700
FAX: 812.336.7790

email: info@solution-tree.com
solution-tree.com

Printed in the United States of America

14 13 12 11 10   1 2 3 4 5

FSC
Mixed Sources
Product group from well-managed
forests and other controlled sources
Cert no. SW-COC-002283
www.fsc.org
© 1996 Forest Stewardship Council

Library of Congress Cataloging-in-Publication Data

Making math accessible to students with special needs : practical tips and suggestions, grades 3-5.
    p. cm.
  "A Joint Publication with r4 Educated Solutions."
  Includes bibliographical references and index.
  ISBN 978-1-934009-67-3 (perfect bound) -- ISBN 978-1-935249-07-8 (library edition) 1. Mathematics--Study and teaching (Primary) 2. Children with disabilities--Education--United States. 3. Special education--United States. 4. Effective teaching. I. R4 Educated Solutions.
  QA135.6.M358 2010
  371.9'0447--dc22
                                    2010013445

Solution Tree
Jeffrey C. Jones, CEO & President

Solution Tree Press
President: Douglas M. Rife
Publisher: Robert D. Clouse
Vice President of Production: Gretchen Knapp
Managing Production Editor: Caroline Wise
Proofreader: Sarah Payne-Mills
Text Designer: Raven Bongiani
Cover Designer: Amy Shock

Acknowledgments

r4 Educated Solutions would like to acknowledge the dedication of the many Region 4 content-area specialists and external reviewers who devoted time to the development of this book. Their expertise and commitment to children produced this resource to assist educators with quality, effective classroom instruction for students with special needs.

Visit **go.solution-tree.com/specialneeds**
to download the reproducibles in this book.

Table of Contents

About r4 Educated Solutions xi

Introduction 1

    Transformational Change 2

    Principles of Response to Intervention 4

    The Goal of *Making Math Accessible to Students*
      With Special Needs. 5

Chapter 1

Why Do We Need to Make Mathematics Accessible
  to All Students? 9

    A Paradigm Shift in Accountability 10

    Mathematics as a 21st Century Skill 11

    Requirements for Math Instruction for Students
      With Special Needs. 13

        High-Quality, Research-Based Instruction. 13

        Least Restrictive Environment 13

        Inclusion 14

    Applying Your Knowledge to Student Needs 16

    Big Ideas of Chapter 1 17

Chapter 2

Creating a Supportive Classroom Environment 19

   The Importance of High Expectations 20

      Supporting High Expectations 21

      Outcomes of High Expectations 21

   A Safe and Focused Environment 23

      Establishing Safety as a Classroom Non-Negotiable 23

      Building Relationships Within the Class and Within Teams . . 25

   Cooperative Learning 26

      Implementing Cooperative Learning Activities 29

   Big Ideas of Chapter 2 33

Chapter 3

Understanding High-Quality, Effective Instruction 35

   The Facts About High-Quality Instruction 36

   Teach Significant and Appropriate Content 39

      Implications for Students With Special Needs 40

      Teach the Language of Mathematics 42

      Assign Relevant Homework 42

   Use Facilitative Questioning 43

      Teach the Questioning Process 44

      Create Effective Questioning Sequences 44

      Allow Adequate Time 49

      Respond to Disruptive Student Behavior 50

   Help Students Make Sense of the Content 54

      Use Graphic Organizers 55

   Assessment to Improve Student Learning 62

   Big Ideas of Chapter 3 65

Chapter 4

Accommodating Mathematics for Students
With Special Needs 67

   The Pyramid of Student Needs 70

   Foundational Instructional Strategies 71

      Teach to Multiple Intelligences 72

Create a Bridge From Prior Knowledge. 72

Use Multiple Representations 74

Teach Problem-Solving Strategies 75

Use Tiered Instruction 78

Supplemental Instructional Strategies. 79

Supporting Students With Memory Deficits 79

Supporting Students With Attention Deficits 82

Supporting Students With Abstract Reasoning Difficulties . . 84

Supporting Students With Organizational Deficits 85

Supporting Students With Processing Difficulties 87

Supporting Students With Metacognitive Deficits 92

Supporting Students With Autism Spectrum Disorders. . . . 94

Big Ideas of Chapter 4 96

Chapter 5

The 5E Instructional Model 97

A 5E Lesson on Equivalent Fractions 101

Engage Phase 102

Explore Phase 107

Explain Phase. 110

Elaborate Phase 115

Evaluate Phase 118

Big Ideas of Chapter 5 120

Chapter 6

Creating and Adapting Lessons for High-Quality
Instruction. 121

Creating a High-Quality Lesson. 125

Engage Phase 126

Explore Phase 127

Explain Phase. 128

Elaborate Phase 132

Evaluate Phase 133

Big Ideas of Chapter 6 134

Epilogue 135

Appendix A
Responses to Tasks and Reflections 141

Appendix B
Reproducibles for Lessons in Chapters 5 and 6 153

Set Model Mat: Halves 154

Set Model Mat: Thirds 155

Set Model Mat: Fourths 156

Set Model Mat: Sixths 157

Set Model Mat: Twelfths 158

Fraction Circles 159

Multiplication Chart 162

Vocabulary Organizer: Equivalent Fractions 163

Fraction Match Cards 164

Performance Assessment 168

Garden Problem 169

Window Pane Problem-Solving Card Station 1 170

Window Pane Problem-Solving Card Station 2 171

Window Pane Problem-Solving Card Station 3 172

Window Pane Problem-Solving Card Station 4 173

Window Pane Problem-Solving Card Station 5 174

Window Pane Problem-Solving Card Station 6 175

*Window Pane Problem-Solving Recording Sheet:
Stations 1 and 2* 176

*Window Pane Problem-Solving Recording Sheet:
Stations 3 and 4* 177

*Window Pane Problem-Solving Recording Sheet:
Stations 5 and 6* 178

Calendar 179

Apple Counters 180

Product Finders 181

Vocabulary Organizer: Factor 182

Vocabulary Organizer: Product 183

The Product Is . . . 16 184

The Product Is . . . 26 185

The Product Is . . . 32 186

The Product Is . . . 35 187

Square-Inch Grid Paper 188

Square-Centimeter Grid Paper 189

Performance Assessment 190

Appendix C

Additional Resources 191

Questioning Sequence Checklist 192

Student Rubric, Grades 3–5 193

Problem-Solving Organizer 194

*Research-Based Questioning Strategies
    for 3–5 Mathematics* 195

5E Lesson Plan Template 196

5E Lesson Plan Short Form 198

References and Resources 199

Index 207

About r4 Educated Solutions

r4 Educated Solutions is a first-choice provider for the needs of educators, schools, and districts, from cutting-edge instructional materials to assessment data visualization, efficient food service training, and inventive transportation solutions. r4 Educated Solutions products and services are developed, field-tested, and implemented by the Region 4 Education Service Center (Region 4).

Region 4, located in Houston, Texas, is one of twenty service centers established by the Texas Legislature in 1967. The service centers assist school districts in improving student performance, enable school districts to operate more efficiently and economically, and implement state initiatives. Encompassing seven counties in the upper Texas Gulf Coast area, Region 4 serves fifty-four independent school districts and forty-nine state-approved charter schools. As the largest service center in Texas, Region 4 serves an educational community of over one million students (almost one-fourth of the state's total student population), more than 83,000 professional educators, and approximately 1,300 campuses.

The core purpose of Region 4 is revolutionizing education to inspire and advance future generations. Instructional materials such as this publication are written and reviewed by content-area specialists who have an array of experience in providing quality, effective classroom instruction that provides the most impact on student achievement.

Introduction

All students must have solid grounding in mathematics to function effectively in today's world. The need to improve the learning of traditionally underserved groups of students is widely recognized; efforts to do so must continue. Students in the top quartile are underserved in different ways; attention to improving the quality of their learning opportunities is equally important. Expectations for all groups of students must be raised. By the time they leave high school, a majority of students should have studied calculus. (Ball et al., 2005, p. 1056)

More than 15 years of research show most Americans and most teachers lack sound mathematical skills, leaving U.S. 12th-grade math students trailing their peers in 21 other nations.

[Teaching mathematics requires] specialized mathematical skills . . . not the same set of math skills required to be a successful accountant, carpenter, or engineer. (Serwach, 2005)

The purpose of *Making Math Accessible to Students With Special Needs* is to support everyone involved in mathematics education in becoming confident and competent with mathematics instruction and assessment so that 99 percent of students will be able to access enrolled grade-level mathematics. High-quality instruction and effective support for students are the most important components in making mathematics accessible for all students.

Transformational Change

Making Math Accessible to Students With Special Needs ascribes to the fundamental premises supported by mathematicians and mathematics educators in both the direct instruction and inquiry learning communities. These premises include the following:

- "Students must be able to formulate and solve problems," including understanding the problem, translating the problem into a precise mathematical question, identifying and using appropriate methods to solve the problem, interpreting and evaluating the solution, and recognizing problems that cannot be solved mathematically (Ball et al., 2005, p. 1056).

- Mathematical reasoning, justifying mathematical statements, and using mathematical terms and notation with degrees of precision appropriate to particular grade levels are fundamental.

- Basic skills are vitally important for everyday uses, and serve as a critical foundation for higher-level mathematics. Students need both computational fluency and an "understanding of the underlying mathematical ideas and principles" (Ball et al., 2005, p. 1056).

- Teachers' ability to help students understand and succeed with math depends on their ability to hear and understand what students are thinking and to explain or show ideas in ways that are accessible to the students (Serwach, 2005).

Making Math Accessible to Students With Special Needs is designed to increase teachers' capacity in making mathematics accessible to *all* students and supports changes in the delivery and support of special education services.

The President's Commission on Excellence in Special Education (2001) had three major recommendations for reform to those services:

1. Focus on results—not on process.

2. Embrace a model of prevention—not a model of failure.

3. Consider children with disabilities as general education children first.

These recommendations are reflected in the No Child Left Behind Act of 2001 (NCLB) and the Individuals with Disabilities Education Act of 2004 (IDEA 2004), which have as their purpose to produce better outcomes for all children and to apply procedures with strong scientific bases to a wide range of decisions, including determination of eligibility for special education in the category of specific learning disabilities (SLD).

Earlier legislation, IDEA 1997, allowed states to mandate the use of the discrepancy model. This model required a significant discrepancy between a student's IQ and his or her achievement to determine the presence of a specific learning disability. Subsequent research has shown the discrepancy model to cause harm by delaying treatment from kindergarten or first grade, when academic and behavior problems first emerge, to later grades when persistent achievement problems are more difficult to resolve (Fletcher et al., 2002).

Accordingly, in IDEA 2004, states are not allowed to mandate the use of the discrepancy model. Instead, IDEA 2004 stipulates that districts may use, as part of the evaluation process for a child with a suspected learning disability, a process that determines if the child responds to scientifically research-based interventions. This process is commonly referred to as *response to intervention* (RTI).

RTI is an integrated approach to the delivery of services that encompasses both general and special education. RTI uses a three-tier pyramid model for the delivery of educational resources, a model that requires a foundation of high-quality instruction for all students. Traditionally, assessment of the underperforming *student* was the focus for determining educational intervention and special education services, with little consideration of the instruction the student had received. RTI replaces this model by first assessing whether the student has received research-based, high-quality *instruction* and then providing for increasing levels of documented high-quality interventions before considering placement in special education. RTI replaces a system in which students are allowed to fail with a system of quick response to needs, a new system designed to prevent problems from increasing.

At the National Summit on Learning Disabilities, researchers (Bradley, Danielson, & Hallahan, 2002) reached consensus on the following conclusion:

> Response to quality intervention is the most promising method of alternative identification and can promote effective practices in schools and help to close the gap between identification and treatment.

> Any effort to scale up response to intervention should be based on problem-solving models that use progress monitoring to gauge

the intensity of intervention in relation to the student's response to intervention. (p. 798)

The researchers also concluded that the traditional bases for SLD identification—intellectual ability, academic achievement discrepancy, and cognitive or psychological processing—were not useful because of a limited or nonexistent research foundation (Bradley et al., 2002).

The language in both NCLB and IDEA 2004 stresses the use of professionally sound interventions and instruction based on defensible research that will result in improved student performance and fewer children requiring special education services. IDEA and its predecessor, the Education for All Handicapped Children Act of 1975, have always required that lack of instruction must always be considered in the eligibility decision-making process and that a child should never be identified for special education if his or her learning or behavioral deficits are a result of failure to provide quality instruction or the lack of access to quality instruction.

To support RTI initiatives, IDEA 2004 specifies that local education agencies may use up to 15 percent of their IDEA allocation to develop and implement coordinated early intervention education services for students who are not receiving special education services, but require additional academic and behavioral support to succeed in the general education environment.

Principles of Response to Intervention

Response to intervention is founded on eight core principles:

1. Teach all children effectively.

2. Intervene early.

3. Use a multitier model of service delivery, exemplified by the student needs model (see chapter 4, pages 70–71).

4. Use a problem-solving method similar to the one provided in figure I.1 to make decisions within a multitier model.

5. Use research-based, scientifically validated interventions and instruction to the extent available.

6. Monitor student progress to inform instruction.

7. Use data to make decisions. A data-based decision regarding student response to intervention is central to RTI practices.

8. Use assessment to:

- Screen all children to identify those not making academic or behavioral progress at expected rates

- Act as diagnostics to determine what children can and cannot do in important academic and behavioral domains

- Monitor progress to determine if academic or behavioral interventions are producing desired effects

Making Math Accessible to Students With Special Needs follows these provisions and supports this legislation. It is critical to ensure that all factors (curriculum, effective instruction, school and classroom environment) have been examined prior to assuming that student factors (or disability) are responsible for student performance. Figure I.1 describes the RTI problem-solving cycle.

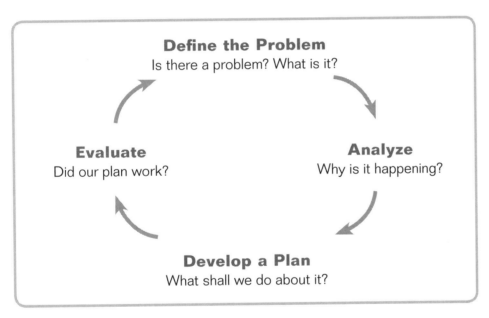

Define the Problem
Is there a problem? What is it?

Analyze
Why is it happening?

Develop a Plan
What shall we do about it?

Evaluate
Did our plan work?

Figure I.1: RTI problem-solving method.

The Goal of *Making Math Accessible to Students With Special Needs*

Making Math Accessible to Students With Special Needs is designed to offer effective solutions for all teachers involved with mathematics instruction, including alternatively certified teachers and adjunct professionals. Each chapter offers educators informed choices for an array of understandable, doable, best-practice instructional procedures.

We will follow four students throughout the book, with opportunities for reflection to increase personal awareness of both the teacher's role and students' needs in the mathematics classroom, tasks to provide interaction with the content of the book, and tips for ideas applicable to real-world classroom situations. Reflections and tasks in each chapter will actively engage readers and can be used as a self-study professional development tool or as a group book study.

The first three chapters of *Making Math Accessible to Students With Special Needs* lay the foundation for working with students with special needs in mathematics classrooms. In chapter 1, we will focus on the rationale and legal requirements to make mathematics accessible to all students, including those with special needs. We will introduce the students we will be following throughout the book, whose needs will be a focus in each chapter. In chapter 2, we will look at creating a supportive classroom environment, which shows how affective supports and a positive classroom environment enhance learning. Chapter 3 is designed to provide teachers with a deeper understanding of high-quality, effective instruction in the mathematics classroom.

Chapter 4 centers on providing accommodations and modifying mathematics for students with special needs. We will highlight both foundational instructional strategies that can be used with all students as well as specific needs of special learners, how these needs affect learning, and specific supplemental instructional strategies to address each need.

Chapters 5 and 6 are designed to connect the fundamental supports outlined in chapters 1 to 4 with real-life classrooms. In chapter 5, we will use a lesson developed using the 5E instructional model, a teaching sequence that meets the needs of students with special needs. The five phases of the sequence are:

1. **Engage**—The purpose is to pique students' interest, get them involved, and connect to their prior knowledge.

2. **Explore**—The purpose is to build understanding by allowing students to actively participate in exploring the concept.

3. **Explain**—The purpose is to formalize students' understanding of the concept to this point in the lesson. Communication among students and between the students and teacher is a key element of the phase.

4. **Elaborate**—The purpose is to extend or apply what students have learned to related concepts.

5. **Evaluate**—The purpose is for students and the teacher to determine if the desired outcome (learning) has taken place.

In chapter 6, we will extend the lesson-planning process by adapting a traditional textbook lesson to the 5E instructional model to make the mathematics accessible to all students.

The epilogue allows readers the opportunity to reflect on the current instructional strategies used in the classroom and identify actions to improve the quality of instruction in the classroom. Sample responses to the reflections and tasks are provided in appendix A. Readers are encouraged to formulate their own responses before referring to the sample answers in the appendix. Appendix B contains reproducibles for the student lessons found in chapters 5 and 6. Finally, appendix C contains resources for the classroom teacher to facilitate implementation.

The authors hope that *Making Math Accessible to Students With Special Needs* will provide useful tools for you to provide high-quality, research-based instruction and support for your students with special needs.

Why Do We Need to Make Mathematics Accessible to All Students?

Our deepest fear is not that we are inadequate. Our deepest fear is that we are powerful beyond measure. It is our light, not our darkness that frightens us. We ask ourselves, who am I to be brilliant, gorgeous, talented and fabulous? Actually, who are you not to be? . . . Your playing small doesn't serve the world. There is nothing enlightened about shrinking so that other people won't feel insecure around you. . . . And as we let our own light shine, we consciously give other people permission to do the same. As we are liberated from our own fear, our presence automatically liberates others.

—Marianne Williamson

Reflection 1.1

Please respond to the following questions. Write from your heart, your beliefs, and your past experience. Then compare your responses to those on page 141.

1. Who are the students in your classes who are not succeeding at mathematics? How would you describe them?

2. Is it possible for all students to learn mathematics with understanding?

3. Why are schools required to make enrolled grade-level mathematics accessible to 99 percent of students?

What do we know about the mathematical proficiency of students? Table 1.1 (page 10) contains the average mathematics scores for students in the fourth grade on the National Assessment of Educational Progress (NAEP). The NAEP included samples from across the United States of more than 168,000 fourth graders. Questions are designed to measure students' knowledge and abilities in five areas: number properties and operations; measurement; geometry; data analysis, statistics, and probability; and algebra. The NAEP scale ranges from 0 to 500. Students with disabilities include those in a special education as well as those receiving services under Section 504.

Table 1.1: Average NAEP Fourth-Grade Scores by Group

	2000	2003	2005	2007	2009
English language learners	199	214	216	217	218
Economically disadvantaged	208	222	225	227	227
White	234	243	246	248	248
Hispanic	208	222	226	227	227
African American	203	216	220	222	222
Students without disabilities	228	237	240	242	242
Students with disabilities	198	214	219	220	221
All students	226	235	238	240	240

Source: Generated using NAEP Data Explorer (National Center for Education Statistics, 2009).

Reflection 1.2

Please respond to the following questions. Write from your heart, your beliefs, and your past experience. Then compare your responses to those on page 141.

1. What student groups are not achieving well in mathematics?

2. Do the NAEP results reflect the performance data of students in your classroom? Why or why not?

3. Reflecting on the fourth-grade scale scores on NAEP, what are the implications for mathematics instruction from grade 3 to grade 5?

A Paradigm Shift in Accountability

The No Child Left Behind Act of 2001 (NCLB) created a paradigm shift in education. School systems are now accountable for the achievement of all students and highly accountable for special populations such as African American, Hispanic, white, economically disadvantaged, special education, and limited English proficient students.

Under the accountability provisions in NCLB, all public school campuses, school districts, and the state are evaluated for adequate yearly progress (AYP), including Title I and non–Title I districts, campuses, and schools; alternative education campuses; and open-enrollment charter schools. Districts, campuses, and the state are required to meet and be evaluated on AYP criteria in three areas: (1) reading/language arts, (2) mathematics, and (3) either graduation rate (for high schools and districts) or attendance rate (for elementary and middle/junior high schools). Graduation rate is included for campuses and districts offering grade 12; those who do not offer grade 12 are evaluated on attendance rate.

If a campus, district, or state that is receiving Title I, Part A funds fails to meet AYP for two consecutive years, it is subject to certain requirements such as offering supplemental education services, offering school choice, and/or taking corrective actions. Regular foundation school program districts and special statutory districts are evaluated for AYP.

One-half percent of students are estimated to be cognitively incapable of achieving at their enrolled grade level (U.S. Department of Education [USDE], 2006). Accordingly, NCLB legislation mandates a 1 percent federal cap on proficient results from alternative assessments. This means that no more than 1 percent of a district's student population can take below-enrolled-grade-level achievement tests and be counted as proficient. Even though a student may be considered proficient for internal school or classroom purposes, the student can be counted as nonproficient for AYP purposes if the district exceeds the 1 percent cap.

In other words, 99 percent of students are expected to be evaluated at enrolled grade-level state standards in order for each school district to achieve adequate yearly progress.

Mathematics as a 21st Century Skill

Mathematics is often a gatekeeper subject that prevents students from graduating or prevents graduates with poor mathematics skills from obtaining better jobs and navigating a complex economy and marketplace. The demands of a more complex workplace, competition for jobs in a global economy, technological advancements, and federal and state legislation have created a need for *all* students to become proficient doing high-level mathematics.

Receiving a solid foundation in elementary mathematics is critical if we expect students to be successful in secondary mathematics and post–high school education. Most importantly, the foundation for all higher-level mathematics lies in the hands of our elementary educators. How can we accommodate the developmental levels of our students and yet create a strong foundation cognitively and emotionally for rigorous mathematics?

Task 1.1

Let's examine one student group, students with special needs.

1. As you reflect on the information on disability categories included in table 1.2, do the percentages align with your expectations? Why or why not?

2. What categories make up the highest percentages of disabilities?

Compare your responses to those on pages 141–142.

Table 1.2: Disability Categories for Students With Special Needs

Disability Category	Percent of Students Aged 6–21 Who Received Special Education Services for the 2006–2007 Year
Learning disabilities	39.9
Speech or language impairments	22.1
Mental retardation	8.0
Emotional disturbance	6.9
Other health impairments	9.1
Multiple disabilities	2.1
Autism	3.9
Orthopedic impairments	1.0
Hearing impairments	1.2
Developmental delay	5.0
Visual impairments	0.4
Traumatic brain injury	0.4

Source: USDE, National Center for Education Statistics (2009).

Requirements for Math Instruction for Students With Special Needs

The major reason for referral and diagnosis for learning disabilities is difficulty in reading (Light & DeFries, 1995). Mathematics has often been an afterthought for students with special needs. The ratio of research, curriculum development, and training in language arts and reading when compared to mathematics is easily 6 to 1 (Gersten, 2002). However, current legislation has targeted services and requirements for students with special needs, and this legislation applies to mathematics as well as reading.

High-Quality, Research-Based Instruction

In the Individuals with Disabilities Education Act of 2004 (IDEA), Congress added new language that all stakeholders, parents, teachers, administrators, advocates, and attorneys can use to ensure that highly qualified teachers serve children with disabilities and that the children receive research-based instruction.

IDEA 2004 (Sec. 601[c][5][E]) introduced requirements that schools provide "high-quality, intensive pre-service preparation and professional development for all personnel who work with children with disabilities" so that all school staff have "skills and knowledge to improve the academic achievement and functional performance of children with disabilities, including the use of scientifically based instructional practices." To say that an instructional program or practice is *scientifically based* means that there is reliable evidence that the program or practice works.

Least Restrictive Environment

The requirement that all students be placed in the *least restrictive environment* was established as early as 1989 (*Daniel R. R. v. State Board of Education*) and reinforced in IDEA 2004. Provisions for the least restrictive environment include:

- Children with disabilities must be educated with children who are not disabled to the maximum extent appropriate.

- Children can be removed from general education only when the nature and severity of disability preclude learning in general education classes, even with the use of supplementary aids and services.

Questions to consider when evaluating whether a student should be removed from general education include:

- Can education in the general education classroom be achieved satisfactorily with supplementary aids and services?

- If a student is placed in a more restrictive setting, is the student integrated to the maximum extent appropriate?

- Is the student capable of acquiring the level of skills normally taught in the general education classroom?

- Is the general education teacher devoting all of his or her time to that student?

- Is the curriculum for that student modified to the point that it is unrecognizable?

IDEA 2004 (Sec. 681[d][1][D]) refined the description of the continuum of alternative placements as "instruction in regular classes, special classes, special schools, home instruction, and instruction in hospitals and institutions." The continuum of alternative placements provides possible settings for least restrictive environments based on the student's instructional needs.

Inclusion

Section 504 of the Rehabilitation Act of 1973 states,

> No otherwise qualified individual with a disability in the United States, as defined in section 706(8) of this title, shall, solely by reason of her or his handicap, be excluded from participation in, be denied the benefits of, or be subjected to discrimination under any program or activity receiving Federal financial assistance or under any program or activity conducted by any Executive agency or by the United States Postal Service. (29 U.S.C. 794[a])

The focus of Section 504 is nondiscrimination. It broadly prohibits the denial of participation or benefits offered by public school programs because of a student's disability. Congress tied the receipt of federal funds to the district's compliance with these requirements. Section 504 maintains responsibility to provide a free appropriate public education to qualifying students whose disabilities are less severe than those students eligible under IDEA. Section 504 is intended to address situations in which individuals are not handicapped, but are treated by others as if they are.

The Section 504 committee—the group of people knowledgeable about the student, the student's evaluation data, the interpretation of evaluation data, and service options—is responsible for evaluation, determination of eligibility for services, and determination of the student's plan of accommodations under Section 504. Eligibility requires a physical or mental impairment and that the impairment substantially limits one or more major life activities. Without an impairment, there is neither educational need nor eligibility for services.

Accommodation plans under Section 504 for eligible students can include seating by the teacher, shortened assignments, and an assignment notebook. As with services provided under IDEA, the accommodations and services provided to students eligible under Section 504 must be consistent with least restrictive environment provisions. Accommodation practices and procedures that provide equitable access to instruction and assessment will be addressed in chapter 4.

Together, the provisions of Section 504, requirements for the least restrictive environment, and the goals of NCLB's 1 percent cap create a pressing need to upgrade the tools and strategies of both general and special educators to work effectively and use research-based best practices with all students. Above all, offering all students high-quality, effective instruction is the right thing to do. No one can foresee the future and determine what our students are capable of and what their contributions to society may be.

Reflection 1.3

Please respond to the following questions. Write from your heart, your beliefs, and your past experience. Then compare your responses to those on page 142.

1. Can we predict what students are capable of accomplishing? Why or why not?

2. How does this impact our instruction?

3. How do the provisions of the least restrictive environment impact instruction?

Task 1.2

Consider the following story (told in a keynote at a learning disabilities conference in the 1970s).

Steven was an eager elementary student, but when asked, he couldn't tell his mother what he had learned in school that day. He described all of the sounds around the room that distracted him from what the teacher was saying. His mother took it upon herself to call the teacher daily and reteach lessons from the class. Steven was diagnosed as having an auditory discrimination learning disability. Years went by with this plan in place, and as the difficulty of the subject matter increased, both Steven and his mother shed many tears at the kitchen table. However, Steven did well enough in high school to get into college, and he did well enough in college to get into medical school. He became one of the few pediatric cardiologists able to hear heart murmurs in infants. His disability is now his pre-eminent ability.

Now think of a student in your classroom who has been unsuccessful in mathematics. Describe the student's behaviors that have caused him or her to be unsuccessful. Use "detective" language—what you see and what you hear—to describe the student.

How do you think the student's beliefs about his or her ability in mathematics affect his or her performance?

What type of learning environment and expectations would best meet the needs of this student? Why?

Answers will vary.

Applying Your Knowledge to Student Needs

As we journey through the book, please keep in mind the student you described in Task 1.2. You will also learn about four other students throughout *Making Math Accessible to Students With Special Needs* and apply what you learn to their needs. Let's meet them.

Rafael has been diagnosed as autistic. He gets along well with classmates. Rafael dislikes math and occasionally makes loud unexpected comments when frustrated. He sometimes takes out his visual dictionary and reads instead of doing his math.

Andy is a student with a learning disability in reading who is learning in an inclusive classroom. He is not disruptive. He is actually rather passive in class, and his former teachers say that he has the ability but lacks motivation. Occasionally he engages other students in off-task behavior. Andy rarely does his homework and either asks questions or sits passively when it's time to do independent work.

Rachelle works very hard in class but doesn't seem to "get it" when concepts are integrated together. She is polite and raises her hand for assistance. Her functional skill level in mathematics is about two years behind grade level. She has been placed in a general education mathematics class. She seems to know something one day but not the next.

Zack is eligible for special education services in the category of emotional disturbance. He often sits by himself and makes barely audible demeaning remarks about others in the room. He is often staring out of the window or drawing pictures. He does some classwork that shows a good level of understanding. Most students avoid him.

Big
Ideas of
Chapter 1

- Significant percentages of primary school students are failing to meet state standards for panel recommendations and commended performance.

- NCLB and IDEA 2004 drive the need to make enrolled grade-level mathematics accessible to 99 percent of students.

- High-quality, research-based instruction must be offered to all students in order to make enrolled grade-level mathematics accessible in the least restrictive environment.

Creating a Supportive Classroom Environment

As long as the differences and diversities of mankind exist, democracy must allow for compromise, for accommodation, and for the recognition of differences.

—Eugene McCarthy

Reflection 2.1

Please respond to the following questions. Write from your heart, your beliefs, and your past experience. Then compare your responses to those on page 142.

1. How would you describe a supportive classroom environment?

2. How important is a supportive environment for student success?

Research supports the idea that the classroom environment influences students' ideas about the causes of success in learning mathematics and consequently influences students' levels of performance, effort, and persistence (Wigfield & Eccles, 2000; Pintrich & Schunk, 1996). Students achieve when they believe that their effort and persistence leads to mathematical understanding. Success begets success.

Additional research has reported that up to 93 percent of communication is nonverbal (Scollon & Scollon, 2001) and that parent and teacher attitudes and involvement affect student achievement in mathematics (Cotton & Wikelund, 1989). A study of 2,580 students in twenty primary schools showed that students who perceived parents, teachers, and peers as supportive were more likely to have higher resiliency behavior—that is, the ability to bounce back from setbacks and frustrations—in communication and cooperation, self-esteem, empathy, help seeking, goals, and aspirations. Providing adult and peer support to primary-school-aged students is a vital strategy in promoting student resiliency and general health (Stewart & Sun, 2004). Student motivation and self-efficacy in the upper elementary grades may be impacted by the degree of adult and peer support received during the primary grades as well.

This research tells us that effective teaching requires the expressed belief that students can and are expected to learn mathematics; our focus must shift from a teacher-centered to student-learning-centered classroom where all students are expected to learn. Student-centered learning strategies create a more positive student attitude toward mathematics and increase achievement (Waddle & Conway, 2005). The more students are involved in a participatory way, the more they will enjoy and succeed in learning mathematics. A classroom that provides a warm and inviting atmosphere encourages participation and meets what are called *affective needs*, which refers to students' feelings and emotions. This chapter will discuss how to create a safe and focused classroom environment in which high expectations are held for all and how to incorporate cooperative learning techniques to create a student-centered classroom to help all students succeed in mathematics.

The Importance of High Expectations

The finest gift you can give anyone is encouragement. Yet almost no one gets the encouragement they need to grow to their full potential. If everyone received the encouragement they need to grow, the genius in almost everyone would blossom and the world would produce abundance beyond our wildest dreams.

—Sidney Madwed

At times, students fail to learn due to the expectations and organization of the learning environment. Traditionally, many educators and parents alike believe that learning mathematics is solely mastery of computational procedures—and struggling students require slow, deliberate, skills-based instruction, and cannot progress until mastery of computation is achieved. In fact, mathematical learning entails a combination of conceptual understanding, procedural fluency, and factual knowledge (National Council of Teachers of Mathematics, 2000). Thus, we must have high expectations that all students will receive high-quality instruction that focuses on complete understanding of enrolled grade-level mathematics and given accommodations to assist them in learning the mathematics beyond computation.

Supporting High Expectations

High expectations reflect the belief that we as teachers are highly confident that students will attend school, become proficient with curriculum, classroom behavior, and other components of the instructional setting.

Students must attend school before any meaningful instruction takes place. Strategies which impact the expectation that students will attend school regularly include: ensuring safety, developing teacher and peer relationships, providing relevant learning and curriculum, and implementing timely interventions (Corville-Smith, Ryan, Adams, & Dalicandro, 1998).

A belief in the proficiency of students with special needs and the value of mathematics for this population falls at the heart of any discussion of high expectations. Standards have been significantly raised for students with special needs. As discussed in chapter 1, NCLB requires that 99 percent of students access and show proficiency with enrolled grade-level curriculum.

Communicating high expectations for this population includes strategies such as calling on students with disabilities as often as students without disabilities, preteaching big ideas or new vocabulary through a relevant activity before classroom instruction or classroom activity, regularly using mnemonics or other memory supports (Scruggs & Mastropieri, 1994), as well as regularly using study guides and graphic organizers. Accommodations provide supports and access to enrolled grade-level mathematics.

Identifying students' strengths and using heterogeneous grouping communicates high academic and behavioral expectations to each group of learners. Integrating supplemental services into the general education classroom and maximizing individual help on an ad hoc basis provides both necessary academic and behavioral supports (Bamburg, 1994).

Assuming responsibility for student learning and communicating beliefs of student competency and value are key to the implementation of high expectations.

Outcomes of High Expectations

A strong relationship exists between high expectations and academic achievement (Marzano, 2003). Schools with high expectations and goals supported by data-driven collaboration and assessment demonstrate high levels of academic achievement (Schmoker, 2001). Without high expectations, students cannot be expected to reach high levels of achievement.

Elementary mathematics teachers have a unique and vital opportunity to lay this foundation.

Task 2.1

Table 2.1 contains a set of research-based strategies that convey positive and high expectations to all students.

Check the strategies that your school uses to convey positive and high expectations to students. Check the strategies that you use in your classroom to convey positive and high expectations to all students. Describe the evidence of this support.

Answers will vary.

Table 2.1: Strategies to Convey Positive and High Expectations

Strategy	Used in My School?	Used in My Classroom?	Evidence
Create personal relationships among students, teachers, and other school staff.			
Provide firm guidance, challenge, and stimulus with loving support.			
Respect students and recognize their strengths and abilities.			
Focus on students' strengths and interests as starting points for learning.			
Convey high expectations to internalize beliefs of worth, thereby developing self-esteem and self-efficacy.			
Provide a rich and varied curriculum.			
Value the unique strengths and intelligences of each individual.			
Structure and organize learning to give all students access to rigorous mathematics.			
Provide opportunities for critical thinking and inquiry.			
Provide opportunities for complex problem solving and decision making.			

Strategy	Used in My School?	Used in My Classroom?	Evidence
Group students in heterogeneous cooperative learning groups.			
Use varied assessment approaches—including authentic assessments that promote student reflection, critical inquiry, and problem solving—that validate students' varied intelligences, strengths, and learning styles.			
Actively engage students in an experiential curriculum that connects to interests, strengths, and real-world activities.			

Reflection 2.2

Please respond to the following questions. Write from your heart, your beliefs, and your past experience. Answers will vary.

1. What actions does your school, or do you as a teacher, need to take to develop a supportive environment?

2. How do you as a teacher communicate to *all* students the belief that they can and, indeed, are expected to understand mathematics?

A Safe and Focused Environment

The cooperative learning methods this chapter explores must be practiced in an environment that is safe for all students and focused so that all students remain on task in mathematics. Two essential components for establishing this environment are:

1. Establishing safety as a classroom non-negotiable

2. Building relationships within the class and within teams

Establishing Safety as a Classroom Non-Negotiable

A graphic organizer on safety can be used to facilitate and record the critical conversation with students regarding safety in the classroom. Consider four categories: physical safety, social safety, emotional safety, and intellectual safety. Direct students to identify *only* those actions to include in each category that ensure the safety of all individuals in the class; this is key to the success of the organizer. Rather than lecturing or telling the answers, use facilitation questions and strategies to elicit these responses and additional appropriate responses. This is a more challenging and instructive exercise than it may appear; it's easier to generate a laundry list of what students are expected *not* to do than of what they are expected *to do*.

Figure 2.1 may provide ideas about what kinds of responses to elicit. Adjust the language in your organizer to suit the grade level of the students. In addition, be mindful of students' disabilities or cultural differences when eliciting responses to complete the organizer. For example, some students with visual field problems need to look sideways at the speaker, just as people with hearing problems may need to turn their heads sideways. An example of a cultural difference would be that some cultures consider looking at an older speaker to be impolite.

An effective closure requires each student to sign a poster of the organizer, signifying the student's agreement in adhering to these safety standards.

Intellectual Safety

- Participate all the time.
- Give help and get help.
- Use actions and words that help everyone succeed.
- Talk only about math.
- Use the opportunity to learn math with understanding.
- Allow others "think time" and time to work.
- Keep the noise level low.

Physical Safety

- Keep hands and feet to yourself.
- Keep books under your desk.
- Walk slowly and carefully.
- Use your "inside" voices.
- Keep classroom materials in order.

Safety Non-Negotiables

Emotional Safety

- Use supportive statements: "Nice try." "I hadn't thought of that."
- Use social conventions: "Please . . ." "Thank you."
- Take the opportunity to work with everyone.
- Give praise.
- Accept praise.
- Value all ideas.

Social Safety

- Encourage and support classmates.
- Know that mistakes are OK (it's how we learn).
- Listen fully and actively when someone is talking.
- Look at the person talking.
- Take the opportunity to work with everyone.

Figure 2.1: A sample safety graphic organizer.

Reflection 2.3

Please respond to the following questions. Write from your heart, your beliefs, and your past experience. Then compare your responses to those on pages 142–143.

1. How would a safe classroom environment support your struggling students?

2. How would a safe classroom environment support all students?

3. What additional support do you need to establish a safe learning environment?

4. What are other actions that would help to ensure the safety of the members of your classroom?

5. What steps should be taken if one or more safeties are not being honored in order to restore safety?

6. What is meant by *non-negotiable*? What are some effective strategies to garner support for the safety non-negotiables?

Building Relationships Within the Class and Within Teams

A well-functioning team is the foundation of successful cooperative learning. In a well-functioning team, members show respect for each other, communicate well, and work together to achieve a goal—in this case, a clear understanding of mathematical concepts and skills. *Team building* is the process of developing well-functioning teams.

In classrooms, the "team" is often a group of students working together. Heterogeneously grouping students results in the most powerful learning for all levels. In a longitudinal study of heterogeneously grouped students beginning in grade 6 (Burris, Heubert, & Levin, 2004), high achievers did better and more students became high achievers as long as the curriculum remained rigorous. By high school, the percentage of low achievers completing trigonometry increased from 38 percent to 53 percent, average achievers from 81 percent to 91 percent, and high achievers from 89 percent to 99 percent.

Heterogeneous groups of four students can be formed with a high, a low, and two average performers. Change groupings every four to six weeks so that everyone has a chance to work with everyone else. When establishing a new group or changing groups, use a team-building activity to allow students the opportunity to learn about each other, including how each person in the team communicates, and practice safety non-negotiables. It is important to use team-building activities that are non-academic and allow everyone to easily participate. Consider using timed team-building activities to set the expectation that some activities have time limitations. An example of a nonacademic team-building activity is Covering the Bases.

Covering the Bases

This activity works well for facilitating student team building. It is critical to start the conversation among students in a nonthreatening, nonacademic way. Trust and academic risk taking are the ultimate goals for a cooperative learning group.

Put students in pairs, and hand out a list of topics such as favorite food, movie, holiday, ice-cream flavor, book, soda, sport, color, school subject, and so on. Direct partners to choose different topics to discuss, working their way down the list until two minutes are up. Reassure students that they will probably not finish the list, and that that's OK.

When time is up, model affirmations that the students will say to one another, such as "Thank you. You are the most interesting person I have met all day." This usually elicits giggles and is intended as a light-hearted, over-the-top affirmation that models appropriate interaction.

Cooperative Learning

Cooperative learning is the instructional use of small groups so that students work together to maximize their own and others' learning. Research has shown that cooperative learning methods result in increased student retention, development of oral communication skills, increased learning and achievement, improved social skills, improved self-esteem, and improved relations among diverse populations (Richards, 2006). Cooperative learning was formally introduced by Johnson and Johnson (1989), whose research shows that when compared with competitive learning, cooperative learning results in:

- Greater efforts to achieve

- More positive relationships among students

- Greater psychological health

In addition, Davidson (1989) reviewed more than seventy studies that compared mathematics achievement using cooperative learning versus traditional whole-class instruction. In more than 40 percent of these studies, students in the small-group approaches *significantly* outscored the control group in individual mathematics performance measures. In only two studies did the control group perform better, and both of these studies had design irregularities.

The power of cooperative learning activities lies in their capacity to create discourse and refine mathematical understandings. Cooperative learning provides a structure not just for discourse, but also for inquiry, reasoning, problem solving, reflective and critical thinking, and student engagement.

Whoever is doing the talking is doing the learning.

Implementing cooperative learning is an effective way to create a supportive classroom environment. When queried whether "anyone can be really good at math if they try," 84 percent of students working in a supportive cooperative learning environment agreed, compared to 54 percent of students in more traditional classroom environments (Boaler, 2006).

Elements of cooperative learning include:

- Positive interdependence—Each group member makes a unique contribution because of his or her resources, role, or task responsibilities.

- Face-to-face interaction—Group members promote each other's successes.

- Individual and group accountability—Group members share responsibility both for final products and for each member's understanding.

For a learning activity to be truly cooperative, these elements of cooperative learning must be in place. Table 2.2 summarizes the goals for each listed element and aligned strategies of effective cooperative learning activities.

Table 2.2: Cooperative Learning Goals and Strategies

Positive Interdependence	Strategy
100 percent of all team members participate.	Keep groups small—three or four members. Reduce size to two members if needed until all students are actively engaged.
	Encourage participation by using an object that is passed to each group member. Only the group member who holds the object has permission to talk. This ensures that all students have the opportunity for discussion. Give students the opportunity to respectfully pass on the topic (for example, by saying, "Pass").
Each member has the opportunity to make a unique contribution due to his or her knowledge, resources, role, or task responsibilities.	Change groups every four to six weeks so that everyone has a chance to work with everyone else.
	Arrange groups to form a heterogeneous mix of students with high, medium high, medium low, and low skill levels.
	Assign the following roles weekly to facilitate task engagement: materials monitor, timekeeper, facilitator, and checker (for understanding).
	Allow students the opportunity to be a peer tutor. Encourage giving and getting help.

continued ➡

Face-to-Face Interaction	Strategy
Students promote each others' successes.	Incorporate a team-building activity for two to four minutes each week. Use a spinner labeled A, B, C, D (or 1, 2, 3, 4) to determine randomly which group member will answer teacher questions during group discussion. Teams need to ensure that each member understands the material and will be able to respond to questions or explain the group's work.
Students discuss and refine their mathematical understanding and skills.	Include structured discussion activities to optimize engagement, on-task behavior, and mathematical understanding. These activities also support linguistic, interpersonal, and kinesthetic intelligences to differentiate learning in order to refine mathematical understanding.
Students connect prior knowledge to new mathematical concepts and skills.	Select activities that allow students to work with team members to connect prior knowledge and experiences to new concepts and skills.
Seating arrangements facilitate discussion and instruction.	Arrange student desks in clusters.

Individual and Group Accountability	Strategy
Students hold each other accountable.	Randomly assign checkers. Ensure that everyone has the opportunity to be a checker. A checker asks other group members to explain the reasoning and justification for the group's solution and strategies.
Students demonstrate their own understanding.	Incorporate the regular use of solo activities like journaling to send students the message that not all work is group work and that they will be assessed individually. Change desk arrangements and/or use privacy folders (file folders opened and propped on their short sides) to give students the opportunity to demonstrate their personal knowledge and skills.
Students make appropriate use of time.	Use an overhead timer. Many students with special needs require additional time to process questions and complete assignment expectations; some students who are given extra time do not use the time wisely or efficiently, however. The timer provides students a tool to pace themselves. This creates a level of comfort for both perfectionists and stragglers. However, teachers must be prudent in the use of timing so as not to cause a harried approach to learning.
Students reflect on actions by individuals and the group.	Encourage reflection on the engagement of members of the group by asking questions such as the following: • How did all team members get the opportunity to participate actively? • How did all team members receive encouragement for their contributions? • How did all team members get an opportunity to communicate their ideas? • How did group members demonstrate active listening strategies when each member was talking? • How were different opinions expressed?

Reflection 2.4

Please respond to the following questions. Write from your heart, your beliefs, and your past experience. Then compare your responses to those on page 143.

1. How do you define *cooperative learning*?

2. How could cooperative learning improve the affective environment of the classroom?

3. What are challenges when implementing cooperative learning?

Implementing Cooperative Learning Activities

Structured cooperative learning activities are important for all students, including students with special needs. Each student—especially those with disabilities—should have a specific responsibility. This approach will allow students with disabilities to engage and feel included during group work. The most effective cooperative activities are brief and used regularly throughout classroom instruction. Review the following activities, and consider which you already use and which you could begin to use.

Jigsaw

In this activity, students are divided into groups. All groups are assigned the same text, and within each group, each member is assigned a portion of that material to learn and teach to the other group members. All students assigned the same portion can collaborate to determine how best to teach the new material before rejoining their original groups to teach it. Individual assessment can follow.

Three-Minute Review

Teachers stop any time during a lecture or discussion and give teams three minutes to review what has been said, ask clarifying questions, or answer questions.

Think-Pair-Share

Participation in this activity uses a three-step cooperative structure. During the first step, individuals think silently about a question posed by the teacher. In the second step, students pair up and exchange thoughts. In the third step, the pairs share their responses with other pairs, other teams, or the entire group.

Team-Pair-Solo

This activity, based on a simple notion of mediated learning, is designed to motivate students to tackle and succeed at problems that were initially beyond their ability. Students solve problems first as a team, then with a partner, and finally on their own. Students can do more things with help (mediation) than they can do alone. By using this strategy, students eventually progress to a point at which they can do alone what at first they could do only with help.

Interview the Expert

In this activity, students first form teams, then the teacher polls the class to see which students have a special knowledge to share. For example, the teacher may ask who was able to solve a difficult math homework question, who has visited Mexico, and so on. Those students (the experts) stand and spread out in the room. The rest of the class surrounds the expert, with no two members of the same team going to the same expert. The experts explain what they know while their classmates listen, ask questions, and take notes. All students then return to their teams. Each team member, in turn, explains what he or she learned. Because each one has gone to a different expert, the students compare notes. If there are questions or disagreements about the learning, all team members stand up to alert the teacher that clarification is needed. The teacher can then take the opportunity to answer any remaining questions or resolve any disagreements with the whole class.

Roundtable

Roundtable structures can be used to brainstorm ideas and generate a large number of responses to a single question or a group of questions. For example, the teacher poses a question for student groups to consider. Each group has one piece of paper and one pen. The first student writes her response to the teacher's question and reads it out loud. She passes the paper to her left; the second student writes his response and reads it out loud. Students may say "Pass" at any time. The paper circulates around the group until time is called.

Loud and Clear

The teacher teaches a member of each team of four a lesson or skill while other members of the class work on a different activity. It then becomes the responsibility of the students receiving instruction to work together to develop a plan to teach the lesson or skill to their classmates.

Throughout the year, all members of the class have the opportunity to act as the teacher. Accordingly, the actual teacher must select lessons or skills that can be successfully taught using this strategy.

Gallery Walk

In this activity, students first work on problems in teams and record their responses on chart paper. A team member then tapes the chart paper on a wall of the room, allowing enough room for other teams to gather around the chart and review the work. Teams walk around the displays, each starting at a different chart, to review and answer teacher-generated questions regarding the solutions. Members write the answers to the questions on sticky notes, and attach them to the chart.

Suggested questions include:

● How is this solution strategy different from your team's solution strategy?

● What did you like best about this solution?

Four Corners

This activity can be used to determine levels of understanding quickly. Identify positions in the four corners in the room as signifying "I completely understand," "I mostly understand," "I somewhat understand," and "I don't understand." Depending on where students stand, the teacher will see if reteaching is needed, no reteaching is needed, or regrouping in teams of four with a member of each group is needed for peer discussion and learning. Safety and trust are critical components for the success of this activity. Students respond honestly only in an environment that they believe is safe—where they trust that they will be treated with respect.

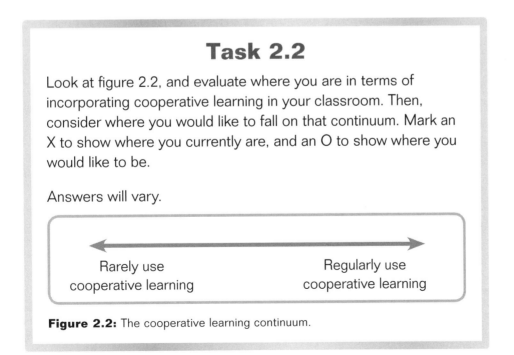

Task 2.2

Look at figure 2.2, and evaluate where you are in terms of incorporating cooperative learning in your classroom. Then, consider where you would like to fall on that continuum. Mark an X to show where you currently are, and an O to show where you would like to be.

Answers will vary.

Rarely use
cooperative learning

Regularly use
cooperative learning

Figure 2.2: The cooperative learning continuum.

Reflection 2.5

Please respond to the following question. Write from your heart, your beliefs, and your past experience. Then compare your responses to those on pages 143–144.

How would a supportive classroom environment make mathematics more accessible to our four students with special needs?

Rafael has been diagnosed as autistic. He gets along well with classmates. Rafael dislikes math and occasionally makes loud unexpected comments when frustrated. He sometimes takes out his visual dictionary and reads instead of doing his math.

Andy is a student with a learning disability in reading who is learning in an inclusive classroom. He is not disruptive. He is actually rather passive in class, and his former teachers say that he has the ability but lacks motivation. Occasionally he engages other students in off-task behavior. Andy rarely does his homework and either asks questions or sits passively when it's time to do independent work.

Rachelle works very hard in class but doesn't seem to "get it" when concepts are integrated together. She is polite and raises her hand for assistance. Her functional skill level in mathematics is about two years behind grade level. She has been placed in a general education mathematics class. She seems to know something one day but not the next.

Zack is eligible for special education services in the category of emotional disturbance. He often sits by himself and makes barely audible demeaning remarks about others in the room. He is often staring out of the window or drawing pictures. He does some classwork that shows a good level of understanding. Most students avoid him.

Big
Ideas of
Chapter 2

- High expectations are critical for student success.

- A safe classroom environment and a well-functioning team are essential components of cooperative learning.

- Cooperative learning is the instructional use of small groups of students working together to maximize their own and others' learning.

- Cooperative learning methods result in increased student achievement.

Chapter 3

Understanding High-Quality, Effective Instruction

Right now we have this little anecdote that goes out that says all children can learn. And everybody really ascribes belief in that. But the problem with that is that that's only half of the equation. The other half of the equation is all children can learn if adults provide high quality instruction.

—Anthony Alvarado

In order to address the conceptual focus of mathematics required for all students, we must implement high-quality instruction. Reforms such as those carried out by former superintendent Anthony Alvarado in New York City's District 2, starting in 1987, have been hailed by education experts as pioneering efforts at districtwide reform and landmark events in the decades-long effort to improve America's schools. Charged with improving the achievement levels of the district's lowest-performing students, Alvarado focused on radically improving the quality of instruction at his schools. He invested heavily in teacher training and sought the best educational practices worldwide. He brought in literacy experts from Australia and New Zealand, the English-speaking nations with the highest literacy rates, to coach his teachers. He held principals accountable as instructional leaders. Alvarado boosted District 2's achievement from tenth to second among thirty-two school districts. Reformers such as Alvarado accelerated the pace of change. "'Tony Alvarado was a turning point,' asserts Lauren Resnick, Director of the University of Pittsburgh's Institute for Learning. 'The District 2 experiment showed what could be done with serious, central leadership'" (Smith, 2005).

High-quality, effective mathematics instruction includes instruction that engages *all* students in the development of conceptual understanding and mathematical fluency. Components of high-quality, effective instruction include discourse, inquiry, conceptual modeling, reasoning, problem solving, critical thinking, and reflective thinking.

Teachers unfamiliar with the components of high-quality mathematics instruction will need more time to become comfortable with the change in instruction. Teachers more familiar with these components will be able to implement them at an accelerated pace.

Research tells us that memorization and rote learning are not as effective for understanding and retention as critical thinking and high-level rigorous learning (Knapp, Shields, & Turnbull, 1992). For students who are gifted, success without effort does little to engage the brain. For students with special needs, rote learning may be challenging, but it fails to make mathematics understandable and, therefore, accessible. For both the gifted and struggling learner—in fact, for all learners—self-efficacy is achieved by effective critical thinking and high-level rigorous learning, and through persistence, hard work, and risk (Bandura, 1994).

Without vigorous use, the brain loses capacity and tone just as a little-used muscle does (Clark, 1992; Ornstein & Thompson, 1984; Wittrock, 1977). In order to make math accessible to *all* students, we must engage *all* brains. How can we do that, and what are the implications for student learning and instruction?

Data reviewed by organizations such as the Education Trust demonstrate clearly that in closing the achievement gap for all students, high-quality instruction not only matters, but is *the* critical component distinguishing between student success and failure. Data show that regardless of a student's background and ability level, what teachers do, what schools do, what districts do, and what states do makes the difference between successful and unsuccessful learners (Education Trust, 2004).

This chapter addresses high-quality instruction for *all* students. In chapter 4, you will explore accommodating and modifying mathematics for students with special needs.

The Facts About High-Quality Instruction

Each of your students arrives on the first day of school with the same number of minutes ahead of them for the year: approximately 180 days

× 7 hours × 60 minutes, for a total of a whopping 75,600 minutes of their lives. For each hour of instruction, your students will spend approximately 10,800 minutes with you. Multiply that times 22 students, and per hour, you are impacting more than 237,600 minutes of your students' lives each year. Now multiply that times the number of years you have been teaching—no wonder teachers are often tired!

And no wonder that the idea of high-quality instruction might seem exhausting; after all, teachers ask, won't that take more time? Clearly, rather than just *spending* more time on teaching, teachers and other stakeholders must *create* more time for learning. In fact, high-quality instruction will actually create time by eliminating ineffective strategies and fruitless pursuits that waste precious minutes. Let's examine some other common fears and misunderstandings about high-quality instruction.

Myth: High-quality instruction means a lot more work for me as the teacher.

Reality: High-quality instruction will shift the burden of learning onto the students, where it belongs. High-quality instruction will transform your teaching and your students' learning. Students will gain purpose and conceptual understandings, and they will practice critical thinking.

Myth: I don't have any resources for implementing the components of high-quality instruction.

Reality: Most instructional resources can be adapted in order to implement the components of high-quality instruction. However, teachers must plan for high-quality instruction by making high-quality lessons a daily priority.

Myth: I can't incorporate this style of instruction because it's not my style.

Reality: High-quality instruction incorporates elements of every teacher's style and more importantly, includes elements of every learner's style.

Myth: Because I know mathematics, I can teach mathematics.

Reality: The ability to do mathematics and the ability to teach mathematics are separate skills. High-quality instruction provides students with the opportunity to develop a clear understanding of mathematics. Research by Ball, Hill, and Bass (2005) has demonstrated that teachers' understanding of mathematics *in the context of instruction* has a greater correlation with student achievement than the number of courses in mathematics a teacher has taken or the amount of time students were given mathematics instruction.

Myth: Good mathematics instruction relies solely on my ability to deliver mathematics content.

Reality: Teachers' beliefs, views, and preferences about mathematics and mathematics teaching play significant, albeit subtle, roles in shaping instructional behavior. Teachers' expectations, mannerisms, and questioning communicate beliefs that affect student achievement and attitudes.

Myth: Direct instruction or "transmission" teaching produces the highest learning gains.

Reality: Using an instructional model that connects students' prior knowledge to real-world mathematics by way of multiple representations creates the highest learning gains. Conceptual frameworks in which explicit connections are made between concrete representations of real-world mathematics and organizational systems like tables and graphs create a foundation for mathematical understanding. Using the organizational system to explicitly connect the real-world mathematics to algorithmic representations allows students to frame a rigorous understanding of mathematics concepts, processes, and skills.

Myth: All students can learn enrolled grade-level mathematics with understanding.

Reality: *Most* students can learn enrolled grade-level mathematics with understanding. Some students are cognitively incapable of learning enrolled grade-level mathematics. These students are served by the 1 percent cap allowed in NCLB for alternative assessment. *All* students, however, are capable of learning mathematics at their functional level. It is incumbent upon teachers to provide students an opportunity for critical, real-world mathematical understandings. Schools are the heart of any society. As educators, we can implement best practices to help develop a competent and confident citizenry.

Ultimately, once we have debunked all the myths, the five "big ideas" of high-quality instruction (Weiss & Pasley, 2004) are:

1. Student engagement with significant and appropriate content

2. A culture conducive to learning

3. Equal access for all students

4. Effective questioning

5. Assistance in making sense of the content

If these big ideas are implemented in a classroom, the chances of a struggling student—especially one with specially diagnosed needs—becoming successful can be greatly increased. As an incidental benefit, all students in the classroom will gain a broader and deeper understanding of mathematical concepts, processes, and skills.

Chapter 2 addressed a culture conducive to learning, and chapter 4 will address how to provide equal access to content. This chapter will focus on the remaining strategies teachers can use to implement high-quality instruction:

- Teach significant and appropriate content.

- Use facilitative questioning.

- Help students make sense of the content.

Finally, we will address the role of assessment in high-quality instruction.

Teach Significant and Appropriate Content

High-quality lessons incorporate various strategies that involve students with significant content by building on prior knowledge and using real-world examples. High-quality lessons are taught at the appropriate level for students, bridging from what they already know and challenging them to do more (Weiss & Pasley, 2004). In this section, we will discuss and examine elements of high-quality instruction that help students to learn the concepts, processes, and skills embedded in standards (see fig. 3.1, page 40).

Reflection 3.1

Please respond to the following questions. Write from your heart, your beliefs, and your past experience. Answers will vary.

1. What concepts and skills are the focus of grade 3, grade 4, and grade 5 mathematics expressed in your state standards?

2. How do the current standards for 3–5 differ from your experiences as a student in those grades?

3. How do the concepts, processes, and skills contained in the standards differ from those contained in the textbook or resource that you are using in your classroom?

4. How necessary is it for *all* students to be proficient in 3–5 mathematics?

5. What implication does this have for your instruction?

Concept: A mental construct that frames a set of examples sharing common attributes

This is the big idea. Processes are assembled to form a concept. A concept is typically a noun.

Example: Place value

Processes: Complex performances drawing on a variety of skills

A combination of skills, processes are typically descriptive statements.

Examples: Order the numbers 98,872; 78,792; and 79,928 from greatest to least. Order the numbers 107,642; 94,216; and 120,130 from least to greatest. Generate a number that is less than 49,408 but greater than 48,534.

Skills: Specific competencies required for complex process performance

Skills are typically represented by verbs.

Examples: Describe each digit in the number using its place value. Represent each number on a place-value chart. Compare the value of digits, then order the numbers.

Figure 3.1: Concepts, processes, and skills.
Source: Erickson, 2002.

Implications for Students With Special Needs

Often, students with special needs are assigned to remedial programs. Many remedial programs are not aligned with the depth, rigor, and complexity of the standards. Too often, remedial programs are characterized by skills-based low expectations instead of high expectations that are focused on significant and appropriate content. Henry Levin of Stanford University notes that for students with special needs, the practice of remediation seldom helps them make it into the educational mainstream. In fact, prolonged remediation causes them to fall further and further behind (Stanford News Service, 1994).

Accelerated Learning

Levin initiated the Accelerated Schools Project at Stanford University as an approach to school change with a focus on improving instruction for students in at-risk situations. He proposes a new type of system in which all stakeholders would work together to accelerate learning by providing students with challenging activities that were traditionally reserved for the gifted and talented. He proposes that all children have the same characteristics, including curiosity, a desire to learn, imagination, and the need for love, support, and affirmation. Therefore, all students deserve high status and respectful behavior from others, regardless of their current ability or circumstance. Accelerated learning includes holding consistently high expectations that build on the student's natural strengths. Research supports the success of Levin's efforts (Stanford News Service, 1994).

Levin's model is founded on the following principles. Note the third bullet in particular:

- High expectations and high status for all

- A timeline for closing the achievement gap (usually the end of elementary school)

- A challenging, interdisciplinary curriculum focusing on student engagement, critical thinking, concepts applied to real-world and personal experiences, and concrete problem solving

- Involvement and empowerment of teachers and parents

Tempered with recognition of developmental levels and needs, these principles lay the foundation for a high-quality learning environment.

Task 3.1

Table 3.1 lists components of accelerated learning; check each indicator found regularly in your classroom.

Answers will vary.

Table 3.1: Components of Accelerated Learning

High expectations and high status for all	
A timeline for closing the achievement gap	
Challenging interdisciplinary curriculum	
Student engagement	
Critical thinking	
Concepts applied to real-world and personal experiences	
Concrete problem solving	
Involvement and empowerment of teachers	
Involvement and empowerment of parents	

Teach the Language of Mathematics

Teaching mathematics requires more than teaching specific content for each grade level. In a sense, mathematics must be taught as a second language. Reading mathematics requires unique knowledge and skills not taught in other content areas. Students must be able to read left to right, right to left, top to bottom, and bottom to top—or even, in some cases, diagonally. Authors of mathematics texts generally write in a very terse or compact style. Each sentence contains a lot of information, and there is little redundancy. Mathematics texts contain more concepts per word, sentence, and per paragraph than any other kind of text (Brennan & Dunlap, 1985; Culyer, 1988; Thomas, 1988).

Mathematics requires students to be proficient at decoding not only words, but also numeric and non-numeric symbols. The meaning is not contained in the words on the page. Instead, the reader constructs meaning by making connections between the new information and what he or she already knows about the topic. The more the reader brings to the text in terms of prior knowledge and skills, the more he or she will learn and remember from what he or she reads. *Metacognition*, the ability to think about and control thinking processes before, during, and after reading is critical to success in mathematics. Strategies for supporting metacognition will be discussed in chapter 4.

> Students with special needs may require additional time in order to construct meaning from mathematical text. Remind students to be patient. Understanding mathematics takes time. They may need to read mathematical text several times for understanding. Mathematical concepts must sometimes be examined several times in different contexts and through different representations before the light bulb of understanding goes on. Have students write observations from their first reading in blue, second reading in green, and third reading in purple.

Assign Relevant Homework

At-home work must be significant and appropriate as well. Create a strong academic culture that convinces students to engage with their schoolwork by doing the following:

- Assign work that is worthy of effort. Offer authentic and engaging project-based work.

- Make the work doable. Assign a clear continuation of well-taught classwork.

- Find out what students need. Make the process of doing the assignment as transparent, concrete, manageable, and simple as possible.

- Create space and time for homework. Provide homework time at the beginning and end of the day.

- Make work public. Display examples that reflect effort.

- Collaborate with fellow educators on content and quantity.

Use Facilitative Questioning

If you don't know where you're going, you'll probably end up somewhere else.

—Dantonio & Beisenherz

Facilitative questioning, another big idea of high-quality instruction, is necessary to support students in learning rigorous and relevant content. Mathematics teachers generally have a clear understanding of mathematics content that is important to high-quality mathematics instruction. Also critical are a deep understanding of the real-world applications of mathematics and a methodology to elicit student thinking and facilitate mathematical understanding. If a clear understanding of mathematics or a methodology that facilitates mathematical understanding is missing, high-quality mathematics instruction becomes challenging, if not impossible. Struggling learners are impacted the most by these deficits.

Parents, peers, and teachers sometimes resort to giving the answers or giving solution strategies to struggling students. This helpfulness is intended to guide the student in seeing the inner workings of a problem. However, giving the answers or giving solution strategies does little to increase understanding for the student and instead increases the student's need to rely on another person (a parent, peer, or teacher) for thinking. A method is needed to guide students in constructing their own mathematical knowledge and developing understandings of mathematical concepts and skills. Using facilitative questioning will assist students in constructing their own knowledge, while assisting teachers in making explicit connections with real-world mathematics and improving their own instructional methodologies.

Facilitation questions guide students in the development of knowledge and are critical for developing or deepening understanding. All students are entitled to the opportunity to develop mathematical understanding. The type of question a teacher asks subtly reveals the teacher's beliefs about his students and his instruction. Does the question reveal that the student is capable of understanding the mathematics? Does the question reveal that the teacher intends for all students to think? For example, changing a question from "Do you understand the lesson?" to "What do you understand about the lesson?" not only shows support for the capability of the student, but also elicits a thinking response from the learner.

Setting high expectations and using open-ended question stems such as *what, when, where, how,* and *why* along with appropriate verbs from Anderson and Krathwohl's taxonomy will support higher-level thinking and mastery of the content in the standards. Table 3.2 provides examples from the taxonomy created by Anderson and Krathwohl (2001).

Teach the Questioning Process

Before using facilitative questions, help students understand what to expect and how to behave during the questioning process. Practice getting students' attention by raising your hand and requesting that students raise their hands. Help students understand that they should "stop doing" and stop talking when they see your hand raised. Consider adding variations, such as raising your hand at shoulder level for the first request and raising it higher for the second request. Offer supports and use prompts such as, "Pair-share possible answers with your partner" and "What one thing do you want me to explain?"

Create Effective Questioning Sequences

The use of taxonomies and classification systems alone, however, will not improve the quality of teacher questions (Good & Brophy, 1986; Reigle, 1976). There is also no evidence that taxonomies and classification systems improve the quality of student responses. Questioning *sequences* develop student understanding more effectively than any single type of question (Beyer, 1997; Costa & Lowery, 1989; Riley, 1981; Wilen, 1991; Wright & Nuthall, 1970).

Questioning sequences combine key questions that elicit high level or critical thinking with follow-up questions that assist students in clarifying, verifying, supporting, and redirecting responses (Dantonio, 1990). Questioning sequences have the potential for engaging students in instructional conversations that deepen their understanding of concepts.

Table 3.2: Anderson and Krathwohl's Taxonomy

	Category	Example	Key Words
I N C R E A S I N G R I G O R	**Remember:** Recall data or information.	Recite a formula.	Arrange, duplicate, label, list, memorize, name, order, recall, recognize, relate, repeat, reproduce, state
	Understand: Understand the meaning of instructions and problems. State a problem in one's own words.	Explain in one's own words the steps for finding area.	Classify, describe, discuss, explain, express, identify, indicate, locate, recognize, report, restate, review, select, translate, understand
	Apply: Use a concept in a new situation. Apply what was learned in the classroom in novel situations.	Apply mathematical concepts to new situations.	Apply, choose, demonstrate, dramatize, employ, illustrate, interpret, operate, practice, schedule, sketch, solve, use, write
	Analyze: Separate concepts or materials into component parts so that the organizational structure may be understood. Distinguish between facts and inferences.	Recognize illogical or false assumptions. Gather information to problem solve correctly.	Analyze, appraise, calculate, categorize, compare, contrast, criticize, differentiate, discriminate, distinguish, examine, experiment, question, test
	Evaluate: Make judgments about the value of concepts, processes, or skills.	Select the most effective solution. Explain the solution.	Appraise, argue, assess, attach, choose, compare, defend, estimate, evaluate, judge, predict, rate, score, select, support, value
	Create: Build a structure or pattern from diverse elements. Put parts together to form a whole, with emphasis on creating a new meaning or structure.	Integrate concepts, processes, and skills to solve a problem. Revise a process to improve the outcome.	Arrange, assemble, collect, compose, construct, create, design, develop, formulate, manage, organize, plan, prepare, propose, set up, write

The goal of questioning sequences is to connect isolated facts into relationships and patterns that form concepts. Effective sequencing involves asking a set of key questions that deal with content, listening to student responses, and following up with questions that encourage continued thinking and processing about the previous answer or topic of study. It is critical to *plan* both key questions and follow-up questions that are based on anticipated student responses. In anticipating student responses, the teacher, parent, or peer tutor must view learning from the student's perspective.

Effective, productive questioning actively engages students in the learning process and is the heart of teaching for understanding. Listen carefully to your students' responses, and use them to understand which questions to ask next to stimulate student thinking. To use questions effectively (Dantonio & Beisenherz, 2001):

- Plan key questions that will create structure and direction for your lesson.

- Choose open-ended questions that use action verbs and focus thinking on *what, why, how,* and so on.

- Ask one question at a time without additional questions or explanation.

- Ask questions at a variety of cognitive levels.

- Use questions that encourage wide student participation.

- Adapt questions to the student's ability level.

- Ask questions logically and sequentially.

- Determine which thinking operations you expect students to use, and ask questions that require those operations.

- Give students a *minimum* of three seconds to think before responding.

- Give students two to three minutes to jot down thoughts for complex, high-level questions.

- Follow up on student responses.

- Encourage students to ask their own questions.

Students can help you understand which questions are most effective for them. For example, direct student groups to write down several of your questions during a predetermined portion of a lesson. Afterwards, prompt each group to rank the questions from the best question—the question that best helped them understand the mathematics concept, process, or skill—to the second-best question, third-best question, and so on. Finally, create a class list of the top-ten best teacher questions. Repeat this activity during student group work to encourage peer assistance through questioning rather than telling: ask students to write down and rank each other's questions, then post the top-ten student questions on the wall.

Questioning is the door of knowledge.

—Irish saying

Learning only occurs with the opportunity for reflection. Questions that promote reflection include:

- What about today's lesson helped you the most?

- What do you think is the most important thing about today's lesson?

- How does today's lesson connect to what we learned yesterday?

Creating Key and Follow-Up Questions

Key questions tap into prior knowledge and provide a "thinking bridge" to new knowledge. Key questions are the initial questions in a questioning sequence that help students focus their thoughts on a given concept. Key questions often help students compare new learning to previously learned concepts, processes, and skills.

Effective questioning sequences also use follow-up questions to scaffold student responses to clarify and refine their understandings. Figure 3.2 shows a series of key and follow-up questions for an exercise in pulling crayons out of a bag.

Order Pulled	Crayon Color
1	Blue
2	Blue
3	Yellow
4	Blue
5	Yellow
6	Blue
7	Yellow
8	Blue

Key Question	How could you describe what the table of data shows?
Student Response	Two blue crayons were drawn first and second.
Follow-Up Questions	How many different colors were pulled from the bag? What were those colors?
Student Response	Two colors, blue and yellow, were pulled out.
Follow-Up Question	Based on these results, would you predict there are more blue crayons or more yellow crayons?
Student Response	More blue crayons.
Follow-Up Question	How could you prove that?
Student Response	I don't know.
Follow-Up Question	How does the number of blue crayons pulled from the bag compare to the number of yellow crayons?
Student Response	There are five blue crayons and three yellow crayons.
Follow-Up Question	How could we say that using the phrase "more likely than"?
Student Response	We are more likely to pull out a blue crayon than a yellow crayon.

Figure 3.2: Sample questioning sequence using pictorial models.

In figure 3.3, after a lesson on fractions using explicit examples, the teacher uses questions with a fraction activity to create more rigorous understanding.

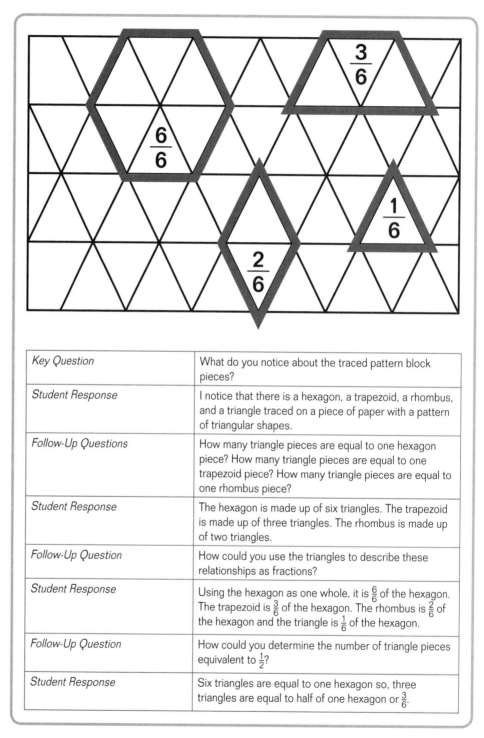

Key Question	What do you notice about the traced pattern block pieces?
Student Response	I notice that there is a hexagon, a trapezoid, a rhombus, and a triangle traced on a piece of paper with a pattern of triangular shapes.
Follow-Up Questions	How many triangle pieces are equal to one hexagon piece? How many triangle pieces are equal to one trapezoid piece? How many triangle pieces are equal to one rhombus piece?
Student Response	The hexagon is made up of six triangles. The trapezoid is made up of three triangles. The rhombus is made up of two triangles.
Follow-Up Question	How could you use the triangles to describe these relationships as fractions?
Student Response	Using the hexagon as one whole, it is $\frac{6}{6}$ of the hexagon. The trapezoid is $\frac{3}{6}$ of the hexagon. The rhombus is $\frac{2}{6}$ of the hexagon and the triangle is $\frac{1}{6}$ of the hexagon.
Follow-Up Question	How could you determine the number of triangle pieces equivalent to $\frac{1}{2}$?
Student Response	Six triangles are equal to one hexagon so, three triangles are equal to half of one hexagon or $\frac{3}{6}$.

Figure 3.3: Sample questioning sequence using pattern blocks.

Use a checklist like the one in table 3.3 to guide your reflections on the type of questioning used in your classroom. A peer coach can help by writing down in the left-hand column questions you ask during a ten-minute segment of instruction. After the lesson, classify the types of questions that were scripted into key questions or follow-up questions. Table 3.3 lists some common types of follow-up questions. Use the completed table to serve as a reflection tool on the types of questions you are asking. A blank copy can be found in appendix C (page 192).

Table 3.3: Sample Questioning Sequence Checklist for Figures 3.2 and 3.3

Question	Key Questions		Follow-Up Questions				
	Question Elicits One Answer	Question Elicits More Than One Answer	Question Clarifies Concepts or Terms	Teacher Verifies Student Response	Teacher Prompts Student to Refocus on Task at Hand	Teacher Allows Other Students to Respond to the Response	Teacher Guides the Student to Give a More Specific Answer
Is pulling out a blue crayon more likely than pulling out a yellow crayon?	X						
Why is it more likely to draw a blue crayon?		X					
Would it be equally as likely to pull a blue crayon as to pull a yellow crayon?			X				
I understood you to say that it would be more likely to draw a blue crayon. Is that correct?				X			
What is the second problem asking you to determine?					X		
Who has an additional way to describe this relationship?						X	
How can you prove that one color is more likely to be chosen than another color?							X

Allow Adequate Time

When giving instruction and asking questions, it's important to be aware of pacing. Ensure that students are focused and attentive during that time by clearing desk space of all nonessential materials and using timed activities to set an expectation of pace.

Next, allow *wait time* for students to respond to questions. Wait time is a teaching strategy critical to the success of students with special needs. The benefits of wait time, formally studied by Mary Budd Rowe (1972, 1987), have been proven through numerous research studies (Atwood & Wilen, 1991; Taylor, Breck, & Aljets, 2004; Tobin, 1987).

When students are given three or more seconds of undisturbed wait time following a question, there are certain positive outcomes:

- The length and correctness of student responses increase.

- The number of "I don't know" and no answer responses decreases.

- The number of volunteered, appropriate answers by larger numbers of students greatly increases.

- The scores of students on academic achievement tests tend to increase.

When teachers wait patiently in silence for three or more seconds after asking questions *and* after receiving a student response, positive changes in teacher behaviors also occur:

- Teachers' questioning strategies tend to be more varied and flexible.

- Teachers decrease the quantity and increase the quality and variety of their questions.

- Teachers ask additional questions that require more complex information processing and higher-level thinking on the part of students.

Extending your hand palm down is an effective way to signal wait time. Rotating your hand to a palm-up position indicates that it is time for the students to respond.

Consider which questions students will need more time to answer—and which students will need more time for any question. Use a think-pair-share to give students enough time to process a question, and allow them to refine their responses with a team member or members before you engage *all* students in a group discussion.

Using a written reflection tool such as a journal will help struggling students recall their ideas for a think-pair-share. In addition, providing a graphic organizer will also scaffold learning for students with organizational and abstract reasoning difficulties, as we'll see in the next chapter.

Respond to Disruptive Student Behavior

During questioning sequences, students may give inappropriate responses that are intended to disrupt the learning environment. The strategies listed here are appropriate for all students, but you may need to consult a child's individualized education plan for further guidance.

When a student gives a disruptive response, pause and look past the student. Use a quiet, normal tone of voice as you:

1. Ignore the response and engage with another student.

2. Briefly respond or redirect while slowly moving closer to the student and asking the original question again.

3. Quietly and privately address the student. Remind the student of safety non-negotiables, or arrange to remove the student from the class.

When giving directions or correcting the behavior of all students:

- *Always* say what you want the student to do.
- *Always* give a replacement activity. If you want the student to stop pencil tapping, direct the student to start writing.

When a student challenges your direction or instruction, model appropriate interaction:

1. Calmly and in a neutral voice repeat the direction word for word.
2. Step away to give the student time to comply.
3. Repeat the direction if needed.
4. Keep your verbal interactions brief, positive, and informative.
5. Avoid sarcasm.
6. Avoid additional conversation.

When the disruptive behavior is severe, such as verbal or physical aggression and obscene or other inappropriate language, take the following steps.

- In the event of physically dangerous behaviors, contact an administrator immediately.

- Create a record of the event—date and time, location, supervising adults, detailed description including what happened prior to the disruption, immediate actions, consequences implemented (if any), and actions taken to minimize future occurrences.

- Contact the student's parent or guardian.

- Establish a procedure for removing the student from the classroom for each incident of severe disruption.

- Compile a list of behaviors that prevent you from teaching and develop a plan to prevent or address each behavior.

Task 3.2

1. Identify a standard that you will be targeting soon.

2. Use the template in table 3.4 to plan a set of key questions that will structure and direct your lesson. Keep the following guidelines in mind:

    *   Phrase the questions clearly and specifically.

    *   Adapt the questions to the students' ability levels.

    *   Ask questions logically and sequentially.

    *   Adapt the questions to a variety of cognitive levels (low and high).

3. Now predict a set of student responses to each of the questions you created. Predict a response for the average learner and the struggling learner.

4. For each student response, plan a set of follow-up questions to clarify understanding and to help students think through their original responses so that they will understand the thinking behind what they said.

Answers will vary.

For example, consider the standard: "Compare fractions using pictorial models." For this standard, a teacher might fill in the first row as follows:

Key Question	Predicted Responses	Follow-Up Questions	Predicted Responses
How can you describe the relationship between the rhombus pattern block and the triangle pattern block?	**Average Student** The triangle is half of the rhombus. **Struggling Student** The triangle and rhombus are different sizes.	How can you prove this relationship? How could you use a fraction to describe their different sizes?	**Average Student** I could count the number of triangles equal to the rhombus, which is two. So, I know that one triangle is equal to half of the rhombus. **Struggling Student** Two triangles are equal to one rhombus. One triangle is half of a rhombus.

Table 3.4: Creating Key and Follow-Up Questions

Standard:			
Key Question	**Predicted Responses**	**Follow-Up Questions**	**Predicted Responses**

Reflection 3.2

Please respond to the following questions. Write from your heart, your beliefs, and your past experience. Then compare your responses to those on pages 144–145

1. What outcome would you predict if you regularly used key and follow-up questions in your classroom?

2. How would this type of questioning help your struggling students access the curriculum?

3. How would the use of follow-up questioning increase student understanding so they can arrive at the answer (instead of being told the answer)?

4. How would this type of questioning help our four students with special needs access the curriculum?

continued ➡

Reflection 3.2 (continued)

Rafael has been diagnosed as autistic. He gets along well with classmates. Rafael dislikes math and occasionally makes loud unexpected comments when frustrated. He sometimes takes out his visual dictionary and reads instead of doing his math.

5. *What questions might you ask that would allow Rafael to use his visual dictionary to complete the math?*

Andy is a student with a learning disability in reading who is learning in an inclusive classroom. He is not disruptive. He is actually rather passive in class, and his former teachers say that he has the ability but lacks motivation. Occasionally he engages other students in off-task behavior. Andy rarely does his homework and either asks questions or sits passively when it's time to do independent work.

6. *What questions might you ask to guide Andy as he reads?*

Rachelle works very hard in class but doesn't seem to "get it" when concepts are integrated together. She is polite and raises her hand for assistance. Her functional skill level in mathematics is about two years behind grade level. She has been placed in a general education mathematics class. She seems to know something one day but not the next.

7. *How might you sequence questions to build on Rachelle's functional skill understanding?*

Zack is eligible for special education services in the category of emotional disturbance. He often sits by himself and makes barely audible demeaning remarks about others in the room. He is often staring out of the window or drawing pictures. He does some classwork that shows a good level of understanding. Most students avoid him.

8. *What questions could you write on index cards for Zack to answer alone when he is not able to interact in a whole-group setting?*

Help Students Make Sense of the Content

Developing understanding is not a spectator sport. Knowledge is a constructive process. The activity of constructing content is what gets stored in memory. Humans don't get ideas; they make ideas. Developing understanding is the foundation of high-quality mathematics instruction; hence, teachers must be facilitators of the constructive process.

Marzano, Gaddy, and Dean (2000) have described a set of instructional strategies that impact student achievement. Table 3.5 lists the strategies and the effect size of each.

Table 3.5: Categories of Instructional Strategies That Affect Student Achievement

Category	Average Effect Size	Percentile Gain
Identifying similarities and differences	1.61	45
Summarizing and note taking	1.00	34
Reinforcing effort and providing recognition	.80	29
Homework and practice	.77	28
Nonlinguistic representations	.75	27
Cooperative learning	.73	27
Setting objectives and providing feedback	.61	23
Generating and testing hypotheses (conjectures)	.61	23
Questions, cues, and advance organizers	.59	22

Use Graphic Organizers

One of the most persistent findings in reading research is that the extent of a student's vocabulary correlates strongly with his or her reading comprehension and to overall academic success (Lehr, Osborn, & Hiebert, 2005). The use of graphic organizers in conjunction with the use of examples and nonexamples facilitates the understanding of mathematical vocabulary and concepts for all students. Table 3.5 shows that the instructional strategy of identifying similarities and differences, including using graphic organizers, resulted in a 45 percentile gain. To support the student with special needs, allow collaborative groups to complete the graphic organizer.

In general, graphic organizers allow students to use short phrases, words, or pictures to illustrate ideas and connections between them. Figure 3.4 (page 56) shows an example of a graphic organizer that helps students develop key mathematical vocabulary.

Concept Organizer

Start with a concept and write it in the center of the organizer. Have students list words, draw pictures, or provide examples to describe the concept. Add those to the organizer, and use arrows to show connections between related ideas.

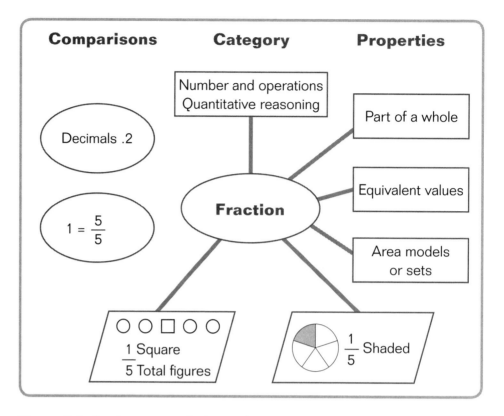

Figure 3.4: Graphic organizer for key mathematical vocabulary.

List-Group-Label

Start with a math term. Then have students generate a list of related words. Together as a class, consider commonalities between the words, and identify broad categories that they can be sorted into (see fig. 3.5).

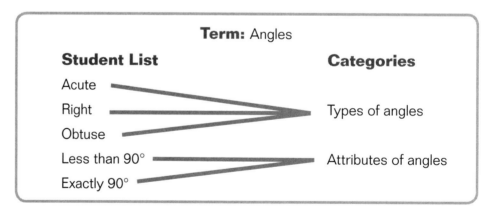

Figure 3.5: Sample list-group-label.

Student VOC

Assign a text for reading, and share a key vocabulary word with students ahead of time. Students then:

1. Write the sentence in which the word appears

2. Predict the meaning of the word by using context clues

3. Find the meaning of the word by asking another person or using a dictionary or other source

4. Use the word in a sentence

5. Choose a way to help remember the word's meaning

Semantic Feature Analysis

1. Provide a table to students with terms to classify.

2. The headings on the table should correspond to the classification categories.

3. Students mark an X in the appropriate category (see table 3.6).

Table 3.6: Sample Semantic Feature Analysis

	2-D	Equilateral	4 Sides	3 Sides
Square	X	X	X	
Triangle	X			X
Trapezoid	X		X	
Rectangle	X		X	

Vocabulary Organizer

1. Students list the vocabulary word in the center of the organizer.

2. Students then create examples and nonexamples of the word.

3. Students use their examples and nonexamples to help them write their own definition and personal association (see fig. 3.6, page 58).

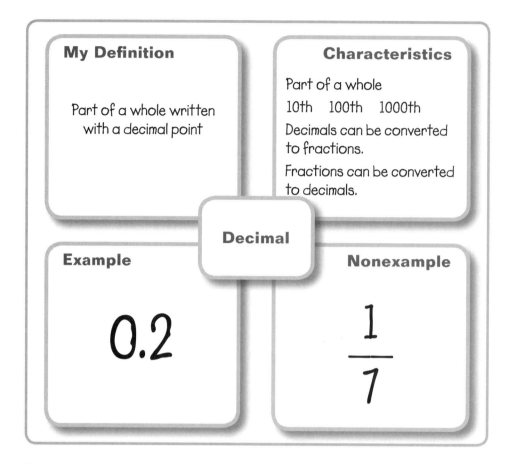

Figure 3.6: Sample vocabulary organizer for *decimal*.

Facilitation Questions for Vocabulary Organizers

How do the properties of the word help refine its meaning?

How do the parts of the organizer help clarify the meaning of the vocabulary word?

Which examples best clarify the meaning of the vocabulary word for you? Why?

What other examples might be helpful in defining this vocabulary word?

Why are nonexamples helpful in defining this vocabulary word?

Which nonexamples are most helpful?

Which vocabulary structure best helps you to remember the critical attributes of a vocabulary word? Why?

Verbal and Visual Word Association

Mathematics proficiency requires a deep and rigorous understanding of the language of mathematics. A vocabulary organizer such as the Verbal and Visual Word Association organizer (see fig. 3.7) supports these understandings.

1. Instruct students to write the vocabulary word or words in the *Term* box, and then to work in pairs to create examples for the *Visual* box.

2. Have partner pairs check their work with other partner pairs. Then discuss the examples as a whole class.

3. Instruct partner pairs to discuss the meaning of the term, then discuss the meaning as a whole class. Write the meaning on a board or paper for students to copy. If students are able to write, instruct students to write their own definition into the *Definition* box. Then discuss the student-generated definitions as a whole class discussion.

4. Finally, instruct students to create drawings or diagrams in the *Personal Association* space, which links the meaning of the term to a personal connection. Discuss.

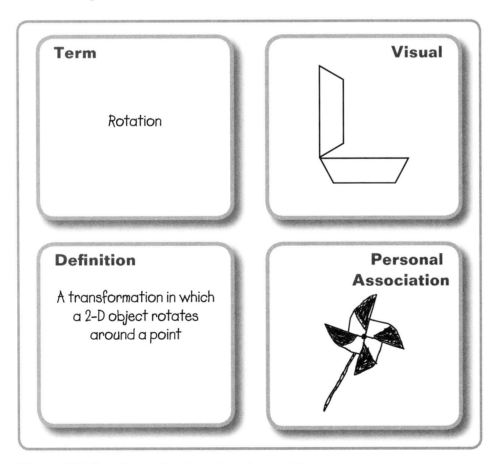

Figure 3.7: Sample verbal and visual word association.

Task 3.3

Table 3.7 contains twelve indicators of high-quality instruction. As you study the table, check each indicator of high-quality instruction that occurs regularly in your classroom. Answers will vary.

Table 3.7: Twelve Indicators of High-Quality Instruction

1	The mathematics content is significant, rigorous, and aligned to standards.	
2	The mathematics content is appropriate for the developmental levels of the students in the class.	
3	Content information provided by the teacher is accurate.	
4	Students are intellectually engaged with important ideas relevant to the focus of the lesson.	
5	The degree of "sense making" of mathematics content within the lesson is appropriate for the developmental levels and needs of the students and the purposes of the lesson.	
6	The pace of the lesson is appropriate for the developmental levels and needs of the students and the purposes of the lesson.	
7	The teacher is able to read the students' levels of understanding and adjust instruction accordingly.	
8	The teacher's questioning strategies are likely to enhance the development of student conceptual understanding and problem solving. (Example: The teacher emphasizes higher-order questions, uses wait time appropriately, and identifies prior understandings.)	
9	The teacher encourages and values active participation of all.	
10	There is a climate of respect for students' ideas, questions, and contributions.	
11	The climate of the lesson encourages students to generate ideas, questions, hypotheses, and/or propositions.	
12	Intellectual rigor, constructive criticism, and the challenging of ideas in a safe environment are evident.	

Task 3.4

Table 3.8 shows how the twelve indicators of high-quality instruction align with the big ideas. Study this table, and assess where your instruction falls on a continuum of low to high implementation of each big idea. Record your answers on figure 3.8.

Answers will vary.

Table 3.8: Twelve Indicators Aligned to the Big Ideas of High-Quality Instruction

Big Idea	Indicators
Student engagement with significant and appropriate content	1, 2, 3, 4, 5, 6
A culture conducive to learning	3, 4, 9, 10, 11, 12
Equal access for all students	5, 6, 7, 9, 10
Effective questioning	7, 8, 11
Assistance in making sense of the content	5, 11, 12

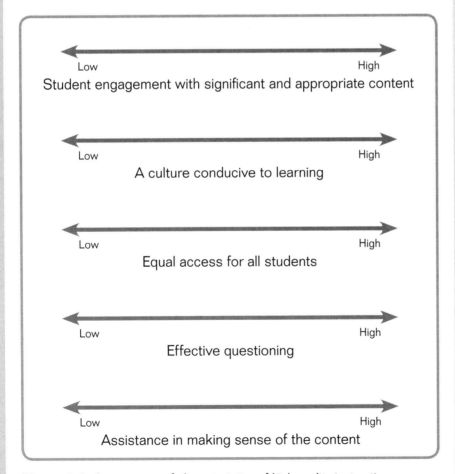

Figure 3.8: A continuum of characteristics of high-quality instruction.

Reflection 3.3

Now re-read the stories of our four students, and identify where your instruction would fall regarding the components of high-quality instruction for each of them. Answer as if the student were enrolled in the grade level that you teach. Write from your heart, your beliefs, and your past experience.

Answers will vary.

Rafael has been diagnosed as autistic. He gets along well with classmates. Rafael dislikes math and occasionally makes loud unexpected comments when frustrated. He sometimes takes out his visual dictionary and reads instead of doing his math.

1. *How much engagement is appropriate for Rafael?*

Andy is a student with a learning disability in reading who is learning in an inclusive classroom. He is not disruptive. He is actually rather passive in class, and his former teachers say that he has the ability but lacks motivation. Occasionally he engages other students in off-task behavior. Andy rarely does his homework and either asks questions or sits passively when it's time to do independent work.

2. *How much assistance will Andy need to make sense of the content?*

Rachelle works very hard in class but doesn't seem to "get it" when concepts are integrated together. She is polite and raises her hand for assistance. Her functional skill level in mathematics is about two years behind grade level. She has been placed in a general education mathematics class. She seems to know something one day but not the next.

3. *How can access to the curriculum be increased for Rachelle?*

Zack is eligible for special education services in the category of emotional disturbance. He often sits by himself, and makes demeaning remarks about others in the room. He is often staring out of the window or drawing pictures. He does some classwork that shows a good level of understanding. Most students avoid him.

4. *How can Zack contribute in creating a culture conducive to learning?*

Assessment to Improve Student Learning

Assessment is a critical step in the cycle of instruction and learning. It is through assessment that we determine the learning that has occurred and the direction for future instruction.

Traditional assessments consist of selected-response items such as multiple choice, true/false, matching, or fill in the blank. Traditional assessments do have advantages: they are easier to construct and grade, and they have one right answer. However, traditional assessments enable students to guess, often only assess lower-level skills, and do not promote critical thinking. It is difficult to determine what a struggling student really understands when guessing is an option.

Performance assessments are assessments in which students communicate their conceptual and procedural understanding of mathematics related to real-life situations by solving an authentic problem. Performance assessments offer students the opportunity to think critically about solutions, synthesize ideas, develop and use problem-solving skills, and reflect on their thinking and the thinking of others. Students are encouraged to demonstrate their thought processes through words and other representations, such as manipulatives, pictures, tables, charts, and diagrams. Performance assessments allow teachers to see and hear what students know.

Performance assessments do take more time to score and require scoring rubrics, but they are invaluable in assessing students with special needs because they allow for differentiation of responses and require evidence of mathematical understanding. Whenever possible, mathematical learning should be placed in a broader problem-solving context and evaluated through performance assessments.

Used together, traditional and performance assessments create a balanced assessment program that measures student progress. Performance assessments allow students to demonstrate their understanding using underlying processes and mathematical tools, while traditional selected-response items provide a measure of students' understanding and misconceptions.

Consider the recommendations from the National Research Council (2000) in table 3.9.

Table 3.9: Assessment Strategies to Improve Student Learning

Best-Practice Assessment Characteristic	Implementation Strategy
Mirrors good instruction	Pick a good thinking problem that you usually do as an example, and see how students do on their own.
Is a continuous, but not intrusive, part of instruction	As students work, check off evidence of learning from a preplanned list of criteria, such as "uses concrete examples to show equivalent fractions."
Provides information to teachers, students, and parents about the levels of understanding that students are reaching	Provide written statements and questions on student work that reflect students' levels of understanding. This will provide parents more information about the student's understanding than a numerical grade.

The Mathematics Performance Assessment Rubric (table 3.10, page 64) analyzes student conceptual knowledge, procedural knowledge, and ability to communicate in a mathematically appropriate way. Use the rubric with verbal or written work to gain a deeper understanding of what your students know, and make decisions about future instruction or reteaching based on what the rubric reveals about individual students' understanding. A student rubric specific to grades 3–5 is located in appendix C (page 193).

Table 3.10: Mathematics Performance Assessment Rubric, Grades 3–5 (Teacher Form)

Correct Solution?   Yes   No

Criteria	4	3	2	1
Conceptual knowledge	**Attribute(s) of Concept(s)** Correctly identifies attributes of the problem, which leads to correct inferences	**Attribute(s) of Concept(s)** Correctly identifies attributes of the problem, which leads to correct inferences	**Attribute(s) of Concept(s)** Identifies some of the attributes of the problem, which leads to partially correct inferences	**Attribute(s) of Concept(s)** Lacks identification of any of the critical attributes of the problem
	Inferences Combines the critical attributes of the problem in order to correctly describe the mathematical relationship(s) inherent in the problem	**Inferences** Combines the critical attributes of the problem, which leads to a partial identification of the mathematical relationship(s) inherent in the problem	**Inferences** Combines the identified attributes of the problem, which leads to a partial identification of the mathematical relationship(s) inherent in the problem	**Inferences** Combines few of the attributes of the problem, which leads to an incomplete identification of the mathematical relationship(s) inherent in the problem
Procedural knowledge	**Appropriate Strategy** Selects and implements an appropriate strategy	**Appropriate Strategy** Selects and implements an appropriate strategy	**Appropriate Strategy** Selects and implements an appropriate strategy	**Appropriate Strategy** Selects and implements an inappropriate strategy
	Representational Form Uses appropriate representation to connect the procedure to the concept of the problem	**Representational Form** Uses appropriate representation to connect the procedure to the concept of the problem	**Representational Form** Uses inconsistent or insufficient representation for the selected solution strategy	**Representational Form** Uses incorrect representations
	Algorithmic Competency Correctly implements a procedure to arrive at a correct solution	**Algorithmic Competency** Implements the selected procedure but arrives at an incorrect solution because of a careless error	**Algorithmic Competency** Implements the selected procedure but arrives at an incorrect solution	**Algorithmic Competency** Makes significant errors
Communication skills	**Justification** Fully answers the question of *why* for the strategy selection, explains the procedure, and/or evaluates the reasonableness of the solution	**Justification** Fully answers the question of *why* for the strategy selection, explains the procedure, and/or evaluates the reasonableness of the solution	**Justification** Incompletely answers the question of *why* for the strategy selection, explains the procedure, and/or evaluates the reasonableness of the solution	**Justification** Provides very little or no explanation of what was done and why
	Terminology Uses appropriate terminology and notation	**Terminology** Uses some appropriate terminology or notation	**Terminology** Uses some appropriate terminology or notation	**Terminology** Uses limited or inappropriate terminology or notation

Reflection 3.4

Please respond to the following questions. Write from your heart, your beliefs, and your past experience. Then compare your responses to those on pages 145–146.

1. What should good assessment do?

2. What are the advantages of a performance assessment over a selected-response assessment?

3. What scaffolding could you use to help students accomplish the expectations of the performance assessment rubric?

Big
Ideas of
Chapter 3

- High-quality, effective instruction is critical for all students.

- Implementing high-quality, effective instruction for all students is doable.

- Research has identified best practices for the implementation of high-quality, effective instruction.

- Graphic organizers are tools to help students learn mathematics vocabulary.

- Well-planned questions are critical to the development of mathematical understanding.

- Assessments provide insight and direction for student learning.

Chapter 4

Accommodating Mathematics for Students With Special Needs

Make everything as simple as possible, but not simpler.

—Albert Einstein

The National Council of Teachers of Mathematics (2000, pp. 12–14) established the following as its equity principle: "High expectations and worthwhile opportunities for all, accommodating differences to help *everyone* learn mathematics, and providing resources and support for all classrooms and students."

Accommodations are practices and procedures of presentation, response, setting, and timing or scheduling that provide equitable access during instruction and assessment. Accommodations are tools that assist students in accessing the curriculum, just as eyeglasses or corrective lenses allow many people to access written material.

Modifications are changes in the content and/or curriculum and performance expectations. Only after implementing high-quality, effective instruction and trying *all* appropriate accommodations in the classroom should modifying the grade-level expectations be even considered. Data reflecting that the student is incapable of accessing grade-level mathematics, along with the list and results of documented quality accommodations tried, are critical in making the decision to modify the curriculum for a student. Modifications or changes to the curriculum can only be made through an individualized education program (IEP) committee and must be recorded in an IEP document.

Both accommodations and modifications are supports for students with special needs, and are sometimes referred to generally as *adaptations*. Regardless of what we choose to call them, we must view them as ways to assist students in accessing the curriculum. Educational accommodations should be made with the intention, if possible, of fading the support over time until it is no longer necessary. For example, suppose a teacher introduces the concepts and procedures of addition and subtraction using real objects and counters (which represent the real objects). Over time, she pairs the counters with pictures and diagrams, and then finally with addition and subtraction algorithms. As the students develop the concepts and procedures of addition and subtraction, the teacher gradually stops using real objects, counters, pictures, and graphic organizers so that students are eventually only using abstract notions to compute. Some students, however, may continue to need the additional support that objects, counters, pictures, and organizers provide, accessing the curriculum through these accommodations.

Adaptations have many incidental benefits beyond their original purpose, and for others than those for whom they were originally created. For example, consider the access ramps to buildings and sidewalks that were required after the passage of the Americans with Disabilities Act of 1990. Those accommodations were designed for persons who utilize wheelchairs or walkers. Others who benefit from these ramps include people pushing baby strollers or grocery carts, pulling luggage, and making deliveries. The ramps were not designed for the convenience of people pushing baby strollers or pulling luggage, but those individuals receive an *incidental benefit* from something required for others' access to buildings.

Similarly, many students who do not have a disability may still exhibit problems with memory, visual perception, attention, or other difficulties. The opportunity for instructional accommodations also helps these students access the curriculum.

In this chapter, we will first present ways to adapt instruction simply by selecting appropriate instructional strategies. Then we will look more closely at specific disabilities and present practical supports that will help make high-quality mathematics instruction more accessible to all students.

Key Questions for Developing an Implementation Plan

Who

- Who will be responsible for preparing the adaptation?
- Who will be responsible for implementing the adaptation?
- Who is available to help with preparing and implementing the adaptation?
- Who is going to pay for the costs of the adaptation?
- Who will monitor the development and implementation of the adaptation?
- Who will implement the strategy instruction?

What

- What previous responsibilities must the preparer(s) give up in order to add this additional responsibility?
- What resources, space, and equipment will be required for making and implementing the adaptation?
- What is the timeline for implementing and evaluating the adaptation?

Where and When

- Where and when will the adaptation be prepared?
- Where and when will strategy instruction be implemented?

How

- How much time will be required for making the adaptation?
- How will the quality of the adaptation be monitored and evaluated?
- How will the effectiveness of the adaptation be determined?
- How long will strategy instruction take?

(Schumaker & Lenz, 1999)

Reflection 4.1

Please respond to the following questions. Write from your heart, your beliefs, and your past experience. Then compare your responses to those on page 146.

1.   What is an accommodation?

2.   What are some accommodations that are used in your classroom?

The Pyramid of Student Needs

The model in figure 4.1, which supports response to intervention (RTI) initiatives, is adapted from a behavioral and literacy model. *Universal, high-quality, effective instruction* is necessary to enable 70 to 80 percent of students to be successful in accessing enrolled grade–level mathematics. *Diagnostic, strategic instruction*—additional procedures—will enable another 10 to 20 percent of students to be successful in accessing enrolled grade–level mathematics. *Targeted, intensive instruction* will be required to enable the final 7 to 10 percent of students to access enrolled grade–level mathematics. This intensive instruction includes additional procedures and additional time. Because the No Child Left Behind legislation mandates that only 1 percent of the student population can be considered proficient when passing a standardized test below their enrolled grade level, it becomes imperative to offer all students high-quality, effective instruction for their enrolled grade level.

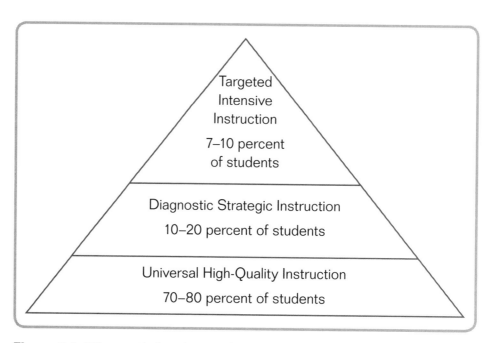

Figure 4.1: RTI pyramid of student needs.

Source: Adapted from Friend & Bursuck (2002) and the University of Texas Center for Reading and Language Arts/Texas Education Agency (2003).

If high-quality instruction were not available to all students, the shape of the triangle would change—possibly invert (see fig. 4.2). The majority of students would be unsuccessful and need diagnostic or targeted intervention.

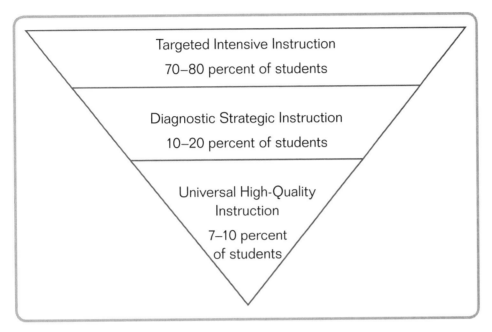

Figure 4.2: Inverted pyramid of student needs.

Source: Adapted from Friend & Bursuck (2002) and the University of Texas Center for Reading and Language Arts/Texas Education Agency (2003).

Reflection 4.2

Please respond to the following questions. Write from your heart, your beliefs, and your past experience. Answers will vary.

Reflect on the number of students who are receiving some form of accommodation or modification in your class, in your school, and in your district.

1. How does the percentage of students receiving these types of adaptations reflect the degree of effective instruction implemented in a classroom or school?

2. How does the percentage of students receiving these types of adaptations impact the proportions of the student-needs triangle?

Foundational Instructional Strategies

Instructional strategies are methods used in the classroom to help make the content comprehensible to students. Learning increases when instructional strategies are tied to the needs and interests of students. The foundational instructional strategies discussed in this section will help many students. Later this chapter will explore supplemental instructional strategies for students with special needs.

Teach to Multiple Intelligences

In 1983, Howard Gardner introduced his theory of multiple intelligences in the book *Frames of Mind*. Gardner (1993) suggests that intelligence is not a single attribute that can be measured and given a number. Although IQ tests measure primarily verbal, logical-mathematical, and some spatial intelligence, Gardner proposes that there are many other kinds of intelligence, including visual/spatial, bodily/kinesthetic, musical, interpersonal, intrapersonal, and naturalist.

Movement is good for all students—and essential for some. Have students move one seat to do the next part of an activity. Some students may need to stand while participating in instructional discourse.

Gardner's theory of multiple intelligences defines eight routes to learning. Constructing lessons that address as many of the intelligences as possible facilitates learning through students' strengths as well as provides opportunities for differentiated instruction. Students can also improve an intelligence in which they are weak.

Create a Bridge From Prior Knowledge

Chapter 3 discussed the importance of prior knowledge as the foundation for all new knowledge. When introducing new concepts, use students' real-life prior knowledge to prepare them.

For example, the area model of the product of a two-digit number and a one-digit number creates a logical bridge to two-digit by two-digit multiplication. A student who solves and explains a multiplication problem in the manner presented in figure 4.3 provides formative data revealing understanding of the area model.

Bridging to division by using the inverse operation with the same models helps *all* students access these important concepts, as illustrated in figure 4.4.

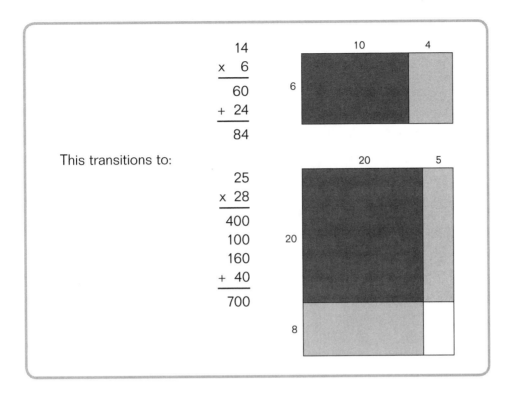

Figure 4.3: Bridging to double-digit multiplication.

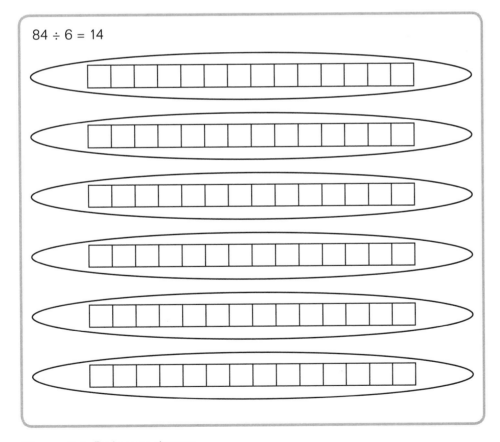

Figure 4.4: Bridging to division.

Use Multiple Representations

In grades 3–5, provide students with multiple representations of a concept. Use manipulatives, pictorial representations, organizational representations such as graphs and tables, and numerical representations.

Manipulatives help all learners and are critical to concept development for students with special needs. Manipulatives are representations of real-life objects and constructs (see fig. 4.5).

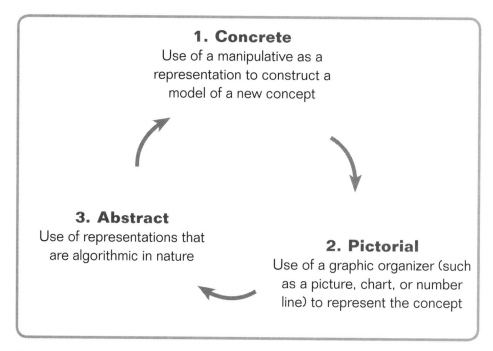

1. Concrete
Use of a manipulative as a representation to construct a model of a new concept

3. Abstract
Use of representations that are algorithmic in nature

2. Pictorial
Use of a graphic organizer (such as a picture, chart, or number line) to represent the concept

Figure 4.5: Mathematical concept development.

Common manipulatives include:

- Color tiles
- Inch cubes
- Pattern blocks
- Two-color counters
- Centimeter cubes
- Solids
- Linking cubes
- Calculators

Keep the concrete representation on the desk when creating pictorial representations, sketches of the concrete representation.

Organizational representations help students make meaning by identifying similarities, differences, or patterns. They help students to make the connection among the concrete, the pictorial, and the abstract representation. Use the questioning strategies from chapter 3 to make those connections explicit for the student.

Teach Problem-Solving Strategies

Solving problems is a practical art, like swimming, or skiing, or playing the piano; you can learn it only by imitation and practice . . . if you wish to learn swimming you have to go in the water, and if you wish to become a problem solver you have to solve problems.

—George Polya

The National Council of Teachers of Mathematics (NCTM) considers problem solving as the overall goal of mathematics education. Problem solving means engaging in a task for which the solution method is not known in advance. In order to find a solution, students must draw on their current knowledge and develop new mathematical understandings. The ability to solve problems is not only a goal of learning mathematics but also a major *means* of learning mathematics. Students should have frequent opportunities to formulate, grapple with, and solve complex problems that require a significant amount of effort—and should then be encouraged to reflect on their thinking (NCTM, 2000). Studies show that when faced with multistep problems, students frequently attempted to solve the problems by randomly combining numbers instead of implementing a solution strategy step by step. Encouraging students to verbalize their thinking— by talking, writing, or drawing the steps they used in solving a problem— was consistently effective in improving the quality of student responses. In part, this process may have been effective because it addressed the impulsive approach to solving problems that many students with mathematics difficulties take. Verbalizing the problem-solving process produced an impressively large average effect size of 0.98 (NCTM, 2007).

George Polya (1957) outlined a four-step problem-solving process in his book *How to Solve It* (see fig. 4.6, page 76). Systematically using Polya's four problem-solving steps helps students carefully plan and monitor the success of their approach while it's still in progress—the way good mathematics students and mathematicians approach problems.

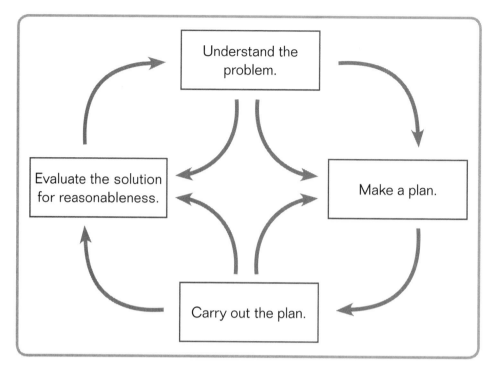

Figure 4.6: Polya's four-step problem-solving process.

Notice that problem solving is a cyclical process. If we've made a plan that doesn't seem to be working, we may need to go back to see if we understood the problem, and then generate a new plan.

A Problem-Solving Organizer

A problem-solving organizer provides a structure for students to use as they solve rich and meaningful problems. By completing the organizer, students attend to the four steps of Polya's problem-solving process. The problem-solving organizer in figure 4.7 can be used during instruction as well as in performance assessments for *all* students.

The most effective strategy in introducing the problem-solving organizer is to model the process using a think-aloud format. A think-aloud activity allows the teacher to give voice to his or her thinking and strategies as he or she goes through the process of problem solving. Following a think-aloud demonstration, give students the opportunity to think aloud with partners before using the problem-solving organizer independently. See appendix C (page 194) for a reproducible version of this problem-solving organizer.

Problem-Solving Organizer

Restate the problem using active voice and simple sentences. (Option: review with a partner and edit.)	
What do I know?	**What do I need to know?**
Which strategy would be useful in solving the problem? • Draw a picture or diagram • Look for a pattern • Guess and check • Act it out • Make a table • Work a simpler problem • Work backwards	**How could this problem be represented?** • Algebra tiles or manipulatives • Picture • Table • Diagram • Graph • Algebraically
Work the problem. Use the back if you need more space.	
Write the answer in a complete sentence:	Explain how you know your answer is reasonable:

Figure 4.7: Sample problem-solving organizer.

Task 4.1

Practice using the Problem-Solving Organizer to solve the following problem. Answers will vary.

The Gulf Pet Store will receive a group of parakeets and puppies for adoption. The total number of parakeets and puppies is 25. Together, the animals have 68 legs. How many parakeets and puppies will the pet store receive?

Instruction in problem-solving strategies must be explicit. Struggling learners lack the processing strategies that successful learners possess. If they

An awareness of passing time is needed to plan solutions to problems efficiently. Use a timer to keep students on task.

do possess strategies, either they are often very limited or the students are unclear about which strategy is most appropriate for a particular situation. Observation and questioning of students can provide important information about which strategies they know and use. Use Research-Based Questioning Strategies for 3–5 Mathematics (appendix C, page 195) to help students ask themselves questions about the problems on which they are working.

Research shows that student explanation of answers leads to greater understanding. Students who explain their solution steps have better post-test scores, are better at providing reasons for their answers, demonstrate deeper knowledge, and transfer their knowledge more effectively to difficult, nonstandard problems (Aleven, Koedinger, & Cross, 1999). Encourage students to explain their solutions, both orally and in writing.

Reflection 4.3

Please respond to the following questions. Write from your heart, your beliefs, and your past experience. Answers will vary.

1. How, if at all, have you used the following problem-solving strategies in your classroom?

   - Work backwards.

   - Solve a simpler problem.

   - Draw a picture or diagram.

   - Guess and check.

   - Act it out.

   - Make a table.

   - Look for a pattern.

2. How often do students in your classes explain their solution steps?

Use Tiered Instruction

Tiered instruction is a method of differentiating instruction to meet the varied learning needs within a group. Create tasks and assign resources according to learning profiles, readiness, and interest.

To tier an individual task, start with a given task for an average learner, and modify it to meet the needs of the struggling learner and the advanced learner. See figure 4.8 for an example.

Learning Level	Task
Average	Explain your solution verbally.
Struggling	Explain your solution by creating a picture or diagram of your steps.
Advanced	Explain your solution strategy with a verbal description. Then explain a different strategy you could use to solve this problem.

Figure 4.8: Sample tiered task.

Supplemental Instructional Strategies

The foundational instructional strategies will help many students succeed. For students with special needs, however, additional strategies may be necessary to create equitable access. They need these strategies to address issues such as the following:

- Memory deficits

- Attention deficits

- Abstract reasoning difficulties

- Organizational deficits

- Processing difficulties

- Metacognitive deficits

- Autism spectrum disorders

Supporting Students With Memory Deficits

Memory has a great impact on mathematics learning, and there are many different kinds of memory. Some students experience difficulty with *short-term* or working memory. These students have trouble remembering new information, copying problems, performing oral drills, and responding to dictation. Working memory is a temporary system with a finite capacity to store arbitrary information. Working memory has the ability to store about seven digits, so it is helpful for temporarily storing phone numbers or facts in a mathematics problem. Working memory increases steadily from age four to fourteen, has a high degree of individual variation, and strongly correlates to student achievement on standardized tests (Jarvis & Gathercole, 2003). Because working memory can be thought of as mental working space, deficits in this area require overt scaffolding or supports.

Other students struggle with *long-term* memory; they have difficulty retaining basic facts and completing problems that involve multiple operations. Students who have problems with *sequential* memory have difficulty telling time and counting money and might also struggle with the processes of column addition, multiplication, long division, or multi-step word problems. They also have difficulty retaining information from a dictated word problem.

Check the signs of memory deficits in table 4.1 that you've seen in your classroom.

Table 4.1: Typical Signs of Memory Deficits

Difficulty retaining rote information	
Difficulty recalling information quickly or easily	
Difficulty retaining information previously taught	
Struggling to complete a task even after verbal directions	
Struggling to write something that has been dictated	
Difficulty keeping up or remembering things	

Table 4.2 summarizes ways to support students with memory deficits. Check those items that you use regularly in your classroom.

Table 4.2: Ways to Support Students With Memory Deficits

Use graphic organizers and problem-solving organizers.	
Chunk information into smaller units.	
Provide multiplication charts.	
Provide calculators.	
Eliminate or reduce copying.	
Provide fill-in-the-blank notes.	
Use fact and cue cards.	
Create mnemonic devices.	

Students with short-term memory issues often have great difficulty copying problems from either the board or the textbook. Reduce or eliminate the need for copying by providing: instructor- or student-created notes; a paper copy of any work from the overhead, board, or textbook; or no carbon required (NCR) paper to a peer who does not have difficulty copying (the peer keeps one copy and shares the other). If you provide notes, use a format that requires students to complete the notes by filling in blanks; it will engage the student and reduce learned helplessness.

Remember, a student's learned helplessness is actually a consequence of the adult's problem: learned helpfulness. In an effort to assist the student or to simply move things along, adults sometimes provide too much information and assistance, and not enough guidance in the form of facilitative questioning.

Other memory supports include cue cards, hundreds charts, mnemonic devices, and calculators.

Cue cards can be attached to math binders or journals (see fig. 4.9). Cue cards are used to trigger memories. They may include pictures of the term or a visual representation that includes vocabulary.

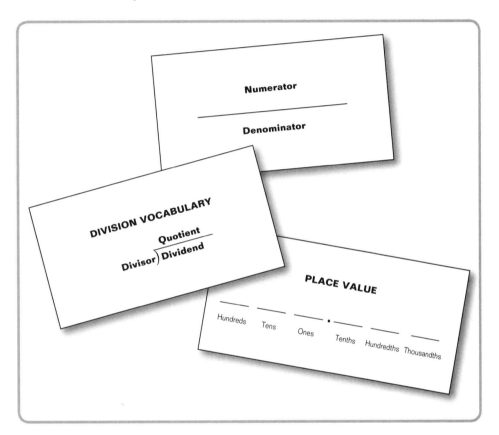

Figure 4.9: Sample cue cards.

Songs can be used as mnemonic devices. Research shows that when students create their own mnemonics their retention is better; however, this method, although more effective, may require more time. Therefore, it may sometimes be more efficient for the teacher to provide the mnemonic device (Mastropieri & Scruggs, 1998).

The effective and appropriate use of *calculators* is necessary for all students and is often critical for students with special needs. Calculators can support computational fluency, as can mental math strategies. Computational fluency—the use of flexible, efficient, and accurate strategies—is an important goal for students with special needs, but the learning of higher-level mathematics should not be contingent on the memorization of facts.

Reflection 4.4

Please respond to the following questions. Write from your heart, your beliefs, and your past experience. Then compare your responses to those on pages 146–147.

1.   What accommodations for memory deficits do you provide in your classroom?

2.   What additional accommodations might be useful for students with memory deficits?

Supporting Students With Attention Deficits

At times, all children experience difficulty attending (attention deficit) or engage in aimless and inappropriate activity (hyperactivity). When these behaviors occur on a regular basis, children may be diagnosed with attention-deficit disorder (ADD) or attention-deficit hyperactivity disorder (ADHD). These diagnoses may reflect too much of a behavior such as fidgeting, or not enough of a behavior such as controlling impulses or paying attention (Goldstein & Goldstein, 1998).

It is estimated that 3 to 5 percent of all schoolchildren are diagnosed with ADHD (American Psychiatric Association, 2000). However, ADHD is not a disability category recognized by the Individuals with Disabilities Education Act. Over half of children with ADHD receive special education services through other categories such as specific learning disabilities, emotional disorders, behavioral disorders, or other health impairments.

Interventions for students diagnosed with ADHD include restricting the environment (such as by seating the student close to the teacher), providing opportunities for active learning, and providing reinforcing consequences (such as praise) for appropriate behavior and nonreinforcing consequences (such as ignoring or time out) for inappropriate behavior.

Attention problems are not always caused by specific learning or physiological deficits. Simple sleepiness can also affect grades and behavior. Lack of sleep can cause irritability, lack of concentration, and rapid jumps from one subject to another—symptoms similar to ADHD. Research by the Brown Medical School and Bradley Hospital shows that "just staying up late can cause increased academic difficulty and attention problems for otherwise healthy, well-functioning kids" (National Institute of Nursing

Research and the National Institute of Mental Health, 2005). When a student is having learning and attention problems, investigate the student's sleep habits first.

Check the signs of attention problems in table 4.3 that you've seen in your classroom.

Movement is essential for some students and benefits all students.

Table 4.3: Typical Signs of Attention Deficits

Making careless errors	
Difficulty sustaining attention	
Seeming not to listen	
Not finishing tasks	
Poor organization	
Avoiding involved tasks	
Losing things	
Easily distracted	
Forgetfulness	

Table 4.4 summarizes ways to support students with attention deficits. Check those items that you use regularly in your classroom.

Table 4.4: Ways to Support Students With Attention Deficits

Design active learning experiences.	
Establish clear routines.	
Make expectations and consequences clear.	
Provide checklists.	
Provide seating away from distractions during independent work.	
Use color highlighting to draw attention to key ideas.	
Keep assignments short.	
Assign a math buddy.	
Reduce the size of the students' cooperative group to only two students.	

Reflection 4.5

Please respond to the following questions. Write from your heart, your beliefs, and your past experience. Then compare your responses to those on page 147.

1. What accommodations for attention deficits do you provide in your classroom?

2. What additional accommodations might be useful for students with attention deficits?

Supporting Students With Abstract Reasoning Difficulties

Effective instructional development of concepts is important to help all students refine their mathematical understanding. Again, making the connection from the concrete to the pictorial to the abstract is essential. Some students may be successful in making the connection from the concrete to the pictorial but then struggle to make the connection to the abstract. Students with abstract reasoning difficulties struggle with organizing and integrating thoughts. They have difficulty understanding abstract concepts, thinking logically, and making reasonable generalizations. Check the signs of abstract reasoning difficulties in table 4.5 that you've seen in your classroom.

Table 4.5: Typical Signs of Abstract Reasoning Difficulties

Not understanding word problems	
Inability to see patterns	
Inability to compare the size of numbers using symbols	
Difficulty evaluating answers for reasonableness	
Difficulty explaining how he or she solved a problem or obtained an answer	
Difficulty explaining broad concepts	
Inability to distinguish important information	

Table 4.6 summarizes ways to support students with abstract reasoning difficulties. Check those items that you use regularly in your classroom.

Table 4.6: Ways to Support Students With Abstract Reasoning Difficulties

Use manipulatives regularly.	
Incorporate higher-level thinking activities.	
Use graphic organizers and problem-solving mats regularly.	
Ask clear and specific questions.	
Reduce the number of concepts presented at one time.	
Use daily think-alouds.	

Reflection 4.6

Please respond to the following questions. Write from your heart, your beliefs, and your past experience. Then compare your responses to those on page 147.

1. What accommodations for abstract reasoning difficulties do you provide in your classroom?

2. What additional accommodations might be useful for students with abstract reasoning difficulties?

Supporting Students With Organizational Deficits

Students with organizational deficits may not only be physically unorganized but also struggle with organizing thoughts, ideas, and information. Disorganized behaviors may be a sign of disorganized thinking. Students with organizational deficits may have difficulties recognizing patterns or sequencing information. They may also struggle with management of assignments and materials. Check the signs of organizational deficits in table 4.7 that you've seen in your classroom.

Table 4.7: Typical Signs of Organizational Deficits

Struggling to keep desk and backpack neat	
Easily distracted	
Lack of time-management skills	
Struggling to understand sequences of events	
Difficulty understanding what to do	
Struggling to classify information	
Inability to follow sequences of algorithms or other procedures	

Table 4.8 summarizes ways to support students with organizational deficits. Check those items that you use regularly in your classroom.

Table 4.8: Ways to Support Students With Organizational Deficits

Require many representations of the solution.	
Use graphic organizers.	
Minimize visual clutter on handouts and tests.	
Establish a clear routine.	
Provide examples of mathematical procedures.	
Model organized think-alouds.	

Graphic organizers are also essential. Advance organizers assist students in understanding mathematical relationships. Creating a graphic organizer (such as that in fig. 4.10) to summarize the information of a lesson assists all students to understand how a concept relates to its different parts. Modeling and encouraging the use of organizers on a regular basis will help all students to succeed, especially those students with special needs. The more patterns and relationships in mathematics are made explicit to struggling students, the greater their understanding and retention.

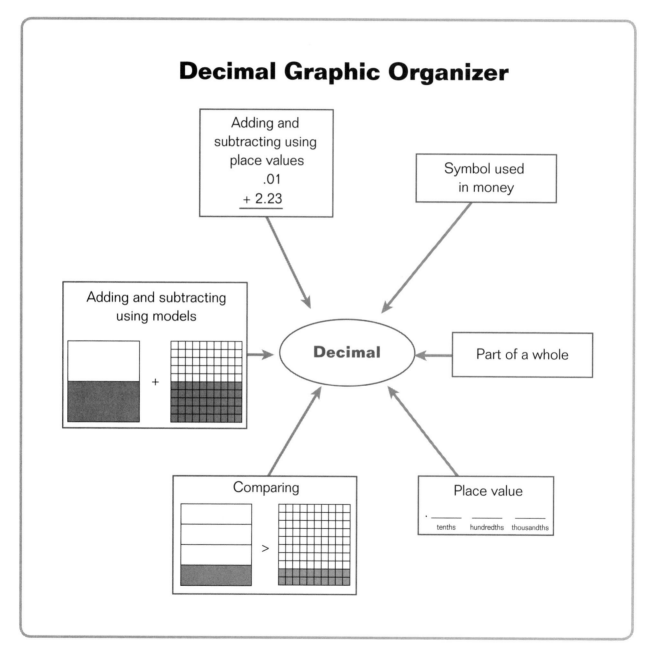

Figure 4.10: Sample graphic organizer for *decimal*.

Supporting Students With Processing Difficulties

Processing difficulties are problems with obtaining, recognizing, and interpreting information taken in through the senses. Students with visual processing difficulties may experience challenges seeing the difference between similar letters, objects, shapes, or part-whole relationships. Interventions should anticipate this confusion and allow time to intentionally explore similarities and differences of words, objects, and mathematical content with the students. Students with auditory processing difficulties may experience challenges discriminating between sounds or similar-sounding words, or recalling instructions given verbally, as well as learning through a lecture format. Interventions may include slowing the teacher's rate of speech, minimizing auditory and visual distractions when giving instructions, and incorporating visual and kinesthetic learning.

Cognitive Processing Deficits

Cognitive processing refers to the process of thinking. Often, cognitive processing includes sensory processing as it affects the thinking process:

> Mathematics is cognitive process-thinking that requires the dual coding of imagery and language. Imagery is fundamental to the process of thinking with numbers. Albert Einstein, whose theories of relativity helped explain our universe, used imagery as the [basis] for his mental processing and problem solving. Perhaps he summarized the importance of imagery best when he said, "If I can't picture it, I can't understand it." (Bell & Tuley, 2003)

Cognitive processing deficits include deficits in numerosity or number sense. Research by David Butterworth in *The Mathematical Brain* (1999) identified deficits in basic number concepts (numerosity) as a cause of difficulties in mathematics. Butterworth describes *numerosity* as the properties of sets of objects that are the pedagogical basis for arithmetic. He notes that the part of the brain that is active during number tasks is very different from the part of the brain that is active during language tasks, and that students with deficits in numerosity show physiological differences in their brain activity.

Check the signs of cognitive processing deficits in table 4.9 that you've seen in your classroom.

Table 4.9: Typical Signs of Cognitive Processing Deficits

Difficulty imagining a mathematical situation	
Difficulty representing a mathematical situation	
Difficulty with problem solving	
Difficulty understanding mathematical concepts	
Difficulty with mental computation	

Table 4.10 summarizes ways to support students with cognitive processing deficits. Check those items that you use regularly in your classroom.

Table 4.10: Ways to Support Students With Cognitive Processing Deficits

Draw a picture of a mathematical situation while verbally describing the picture.	
Have students use manipulatives to model a problem, and ask questions that connect the model to the mathematical situation, such as "How does each part of your model represent each part of the situation?"	
Use a think-aloud, which allows students to see and hear the process of problem solving.	
Use a problem-solving organizer.	
Connect real-life mathematical situations first to a model, then to organizational systems such as diagrams, tables, and graphs, and finally to an algorithm.	
Use of place-value charts and other resources that allow students to see the patterns in computation frameworks.	

Support for these learners includes instruction in a strong conceptual understanding of mathematical patterns and relationships and using teachable moments to correct misconceptions. Planning and implementing lessons that intentionally bridge among the concrete, the organizational, and abstract representations in mathematics and using organizers that help to connect mathematical content will also provide cognitive processing support.

Reflection 4.8

Please respond to the following questions. Write from your heart, your beliefs, and your past experience. Then compare your responses to those on page 147.

1. What accommodations for cognitive processing deficits do you provide in your classroom?

2. What additional accommodations might be useful for students with cognitive processing deficits?

Visual Processing Deficits

Students with visual processing deficits have trouble understanding information presented visually. Visual processing deficits can be organized into figure-ground, visual discrimination, reversal, and spatial orientation deficiencies. Difficulties with *figure-ground* processing include trouble seeing an image within a competing background or picking one line of print from another while reading or following math sequences. Using an index card or marker will help to blot out distractors. Students with *visual discrimination* difficulties have trouble seeing the difference between two similar objects. Use uncluttered worksheets with ample white space and large, sans-serif fonts, which have fewer embellishments, such as Arial size 24. Color-coding may also help; consider using different colors to indicate place value, for example (one color for ones, another for tens, and another for hundreds). Color-coding could help students observe the pattern for each period. (Since 6 percent of males of European ancestry have red-green color blindness, use colors other than red and green.) *Reversals* in reading can result from difficulties in consistently tracking from left to right, and in mathematics, doing operations that require tracking from right to left. Strategies such as using index cards to cover and gradually reveal information only as it is needed may help students with reversals in reading. Students who have *spatial orientation* difficulties lose materials, produce unorganized work, and sometimes have difficulty judging time. Using graphic organizers and timers will scaffold organization for this group of students.

Check the signs of visual processing deficits in table 4.11 (page 90) that you've seen in your classroom.

Table 4.11: Typical Signs of Visual Processing Deficits

Losing his or her place on a page	
Difficulty copying	
Struggling to differentiate mathematical signs (=, +, −)	
Misjudging speed and distance	
Difficulty discriminating objects in a picture	
Difficulty gaining information from maps, pictures, charts, or graphs	

Table 4.12 summarizes ways to support students with visual processing deficits. Check those items that you use regularly in your classroom.

Table 4.12: Ways to Support Students With Visual Processing Deficits

Use an index card or marker to hide irrelevant information.	
Use large fonts and wide spacing on handouts.	
Give assignments in pieces or sections.	
Reduce or eliminate copying.	
Use color-coding to reinforce concepts.	
Always speak the numbers in problems rather than just pointing to a written problem.	
Use paper with dark lines or grids instead of standard paper with light blue lines.	
Use a card with a "window" cut out so that only a small amount of information is seen (see fig. 4.11).	
Adapt written assignments by enlarging the print and placing fewer problems on a page.	
Use manipulatives.	
Use graphic organizers.	

Some students have trouble discriminating the item number from the text of the problem itself. These students may need to hide the number of the problem to prevent confusion (see fig. 4.11).

Reflection 4.9

Please respond to the following questions. Write from your heart, your beliefs, and your past experience. Then compare your responses to those on pages 147–148.

1. What accommodations for visual processing deficits do you provide in your classroom?

2. What additional accommodations might be useful for students with visual processing deficits?

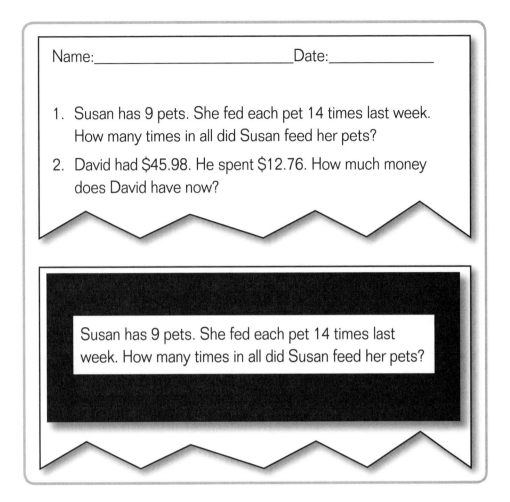

Name:_____Date:_____

1. Susan has 9 pets. She fed each pet 14 times last week. How many times in all did Susan feed her pets?

2. David had $45.98. He spent $12.76. How much money does David have now?

Susan has 9 pets. She fed each pet 14 times last week. How many times in all did Susan feed her pets?

Figure 4.11: Sample window cutout.

Auditory Processing Deficits

As discussed earlier, students with auditory processing difficulties may experience challenges discriminating between sounds, rhyming words, or recalling instructions given verbally, as well as learning through a lecture format. Students with auditory deficits in the *figure-ground* category may have difficulty attending because they cannot filter out extraneous noise. Students with auditory deficits in *discrimination* may be unable to distinguish between spoken words such as *thirteen* and *thirty* (this could also be a language issue). Students with auditory deficits in *spatial organization* may have trouble following multiple directions.

Check the signs of auditory processing deficits in table 4.13 (page 92) that you've seen in your classroom.

Table 4.13: Typical Signs of Auditory Processing Deficits

Difficulty following dictated assignments or oral directions	
Struggling with orally posed questions or drills	
Difficulty paying attention in class	
Struggling to follow classroom discussion	
Misinterpreting spoken information	

Table 4.14 summarizes ways to support students with auditory processing deficits. Check those items that you use regularly in your classroom.

Table 4.14: Ways to Support Students With Auditory Processing Deficits

Provide oral and written directions and notes.	
Seat the student near the teacher.	
Repeat main ideas.	
Assign a reading buddy to read and/or clarify directions.	
Use a slower rate of speech.	
Review vocabulary.	

Reflection 4.10

Please respond to the following questions. Write from your heart, your beliefs, and your past experience. Then compare your responses to those on page 148.

1. What accommodations for auditory processing deficits do you provide in your classroom?

2. What additional accommodations might be useful for students with auditory processing deficits?

Supporting Students With Metacognitive Deficits

Metacognition, or thinking about one's thinking, is a weak skill for many students and is often lacking in students with special needs. Metacognition consists of two basic processes occurring simultaneously: *monitoring your progress* as you learn, and *making changes and adapting* your strategies if you perceive you are not doing so well (Winn & Snyder, 1996). Students gain confidence and become more independent learners as they develop metacognitive strategies. The development of independence and personal advocacy through self-knowledge is important for all students but critical for students with special needs. Scaffold this important skill by providing a structure for metacognition in the form of reflective journals, self-questioning, and think-aloud exercises.

Check the signs of metacognitive deficits in table 4.15 that you've seen in your classroom.

Table 4.15: Typical Signs of Metacognitive Deficits

Difficulty identifying and selecting appropriate strategies	
Struggling to generalize or organize information	
Struggling to evaluate answers for accuracy	
Difficulty monitoring his or her ability to solve problems	
Struggling to explain how he or she arrived at a solution	

Table 4.16 summarizes ways to support students with metacognitive deficits. Check those items that you use regularly in your classroom.

Table 4.16: Ways to Support Students With Metacognitive Deficits

Provide explicit instruction in problem-solving strategies.	
Model the appropriate use of strategies.	
Teach steps to problem solving.	
Provide visuals.	
Demonstrate multiple strategies when problem solving.	
Use self-questioning.	
Use think-aloud exercises.	
Use graphic organizers and graphic models.	
Use journal writing that focuses on explaining thinking, reflecting on reasonableness of solutions, and so on.	

Reflection 4.11

Please respond to the following questions. Write from your heart, your beliefs, and your past experience. Then compare your responses to those on page 148.

1. What accommodations for metacognitive deficits do you provide in your classroom?

2. What additional accommodations might be useful for students with metacognitive deficits?

Supporting Students With Autism Spectrum Disorders

Autism spectrum disorders (ASD) include Asperger's syndrome, pervasive development disorder not otherwise specified (PDD-NOS), and autism. Autism spectrum disorders are characterized by a delay in social communication and language, as well as by self-stimulatory and aggressive behavior. Each child with an autism spectrum disorder presents a unique collage of strengths and needs (Freeman, 1997). Pervasive developmental disorder (PDD) is a category of disorders, but not a diagnostic label. Individuals with PDD tend to lack curiosity about their environment, have difficulty with changes in routines, and display consistent unusual behaviors that are present in all settings.

The performance of students with ASD is somewhat uneven. Students often excel in either quantitative or verbal areas, but not both. Individuals with ASD may offer resistance to new situations more often than the neurotypical population.

A student with ASD has receptive language difficulties. Many times, the student cannot understand language as well as a teacher believes he or she can, causing the student to demonstrate aggressive behavior or lack of initiative. The student may lack the language necessary to communicate his or her needs appropriately. Providing visual examples whenever possible, along with a verbal description, is not only good teaching, but also allows ASD students access to the curriculum and important information for daily classroom tasks, routines, and procedures.

Templates that act as visual examples when describing information or expectations provide a necessary accommodation. For example, display a set of representations at the front of the room, and point to it when speaking. The student can also keep a template or visual example of the verbal description in his or her binder.

High-functioning individuals with autism (HFIWA) may need accommodations in the primary school mathematics classroom not only to feel safe, but also to access the curriculum. Structuring the environment through visual cues creates a sense of safety and helps students understand procedures. Remember that accommodations will have incidental benefits for students who do not have autism: "Similarities between the challenges facing HFIWA and their neurotypical counterparts are perhaps greater than the differences . . . nevertheless, [individuals] on the autistic spectrum do face challenges which are frequently qualitatively different and may take on greater magnitude" (Perner, 2002).

Table 4.17 lists signs that a student with ASD may exhibit. Mark those you have seen in students you know to have ASD.

Table 4.17: Typical Signs of Autism Spectrum Disorders

Preferring to work independently	
Seeming to "tune out" others	
Difficulty with changes in the schedule and transitions	
Spending a lot of time organizing or lining up objects	
Showing unusual attachment to objects	
Difficulty interacting and communicating with others appropriately	

Table 4.18 summarizes ways to support students with ASD. Check those items that you use regularly in your classroom.

Table 4.18: Ways to Support Students With Autism Spectrum Disorders

Obtain the student's attention before giving directions.	
Pair verbal language with gestures and visuals.	
Print clear and explicit directions in writing.	
Provide materials for the student to work independently.	
Provide ample assistance to complete a task successfully.	
Provide clear feedback regarding correct and incorrect responses and behaviors.	
Give clear and immediate consequences and reinforcers.	
Schedule explicit break times.	
Follow unpreferred activities with preferred activities.	
Locate work areas in the least distracting settings, and mark them so that the student can find his or her own way.	
Ensure easy visual access by the teacher.	
Provide clear transition signals and assistance during transitions.	

Reflection 4.12

Please respond to the following questions. Write from your heart, your beliefs, and your past experience. Then compare your responses to those on page 148.

1. What accommodations for autism spectrum disorders do you provide in your classroom?

2. What additional accommodations might be useful for students with autism spectrum disorders?

Foundational instructional strategies assist all students in accessing the grade-level curriculum. These are strategies to be embedded throughout daily instruction if we are to help 70–80 percent of students be successful in Tier 1 instruction. For students who continue to exhibit struggles in the classroom, additional supplemental instructional strategies can be implemented. Several of the strategies, such as graphic organizers, the use of manipulatives, and think-alouds appear several times. Incorporate the use of these strategies in planning instruction to impact the largest number of students, and work to incorporate other strategies as needed.

Big
Ideas of
Chapter 4

- Accommodations are tools that assist students in accessing the curriculum.

- Modifications are changes in the content and/or curriculum and performance expectations.

- Foundational instructional strategies that support all learners include teaching to multiple intelligences, creating a bridge from prior knowledge, using multiple representations, teaching problem solving, and using tiered instruction.

- Supplemental instructional strategies are used to support equitable access for students with special needs.

- Graphic organizers, think-alouds, and the use of manipulatives are examples of supplemental instructional strategies that support more than one type of student learning deficit.

The 5E Instructional Model

Students must learn mathematics with understanding, actively building new knowledge from experience and prior knowledge.

—National Council of Teachers of Mathematics

If I have seen farther, it is by standing on the shoulders of giants.

—Isaac Newton

An effective lesson that provides the most impact on student achievement ensures that students are actively engaged in learning as well as reflecting on their learning to make sense of the activities. Learning something new or understanding something familiar in greater depth involves making sense of both our prior experiences and firsthand knowledge gained from new explorations. An effective lesson provides opportunities to use, extend, and apply what is learned.

The Five E (5E) instructional model is a research-based lesson cycle that has been shown to increase student achievement. The 5E model was originally developed as a framework for developing inquiry-based lessons for science educators. However, because mathematics educators are embracing an inquiry approach to mathematics instruction, the 5E model can be used to implement high-quality, effective instruction for mathematics as well.

The 5E instructional model developed by Roger W. Bybee, past executive director of the National Research Council and the Center for

Science, Mathematics, and Engineering Education, provides such a model (Trowbridge & Bybee, 1996). CSMEE was established in 1995 to provide coordination of all of the National Research Council's education activities and reform efforts for students at all levels, specifically those in kindergarten through twelfth grade, undergraduate institutions, school-to-work programs, and continuing education.

This research-based model meets the requirements of effective instruction and has unique benefits for all students, particularly students with special needs. This model is an inquiry-based learning cycle that:

- Puts the responsibility for learning squarely where it belongs—on the shoulders of the student

- Facilitates learning more effectively for a broader range of students than traditional lecture-first strategies

- Promotes greater retention of the subject matter than traditional strategies

The 5E model incorporates effective teaching strategies including problem solving, facilitative questioning, questioning sequences, vocabulary development, and rich, meaningful assessment techniques. The 5E model addresses Gardner's multiple intelligences and incorporates many of the identified best practices for mathematics instruction.

The components of the 5E instructional model are the following:

1. **Engage**—The Engage phase should arouse curiosity, show students the focus of the lesson, and provide the teacher with information on the students' background knowledge. The teacher initiates this stage by asking well-chosen questions, defining a problem to be solved, or showing something intriguing. The activity should be designed to interest students in the problem, to make connections to past and present learning, and to build common background.

2. **Explore**—The Explore phase is the bulk of the lesson. It directly involves students with the key concepts of the lesson through guided exploration and hands-on activities that require them to probe, inquire, and question. As we learn, the puzzle pieces—the ideas and concepts necessary to solve the problem—begin to fit together or need to be broken down and reconstructed several times. In this stage, the teacher observes and listens to students as they interact with each other and the activity. The teacher

asks probing facilitation questions to help students clarify their understanding of major concepts and redirect the questions when necessary.

3. **Explain**—In the Explain phase, the teacher asks questions to help lead students from the concrete to the abstract and from the known to the new. Students should work in small groups as they begin to sequence logically events and facts from the investigation and communicate these findings to each other and the teacher. Acting as a facilitator, the teacher uses this phase to offer further explanations and provide additional meaning or information, and to formalize conceptual vocabulary. Giving labels or correct terminology is far more meaningful and helpful in retention if it is done after the learner has had a direct experience. The explanation stage is used to record the learner's development and grasp of the key ideas and concepts of the lesson.

4. **Elaborate**—The Elaborate phase allows students to extend and expand what they have learned in the first three phases, connect this knowledge with their prior learning to create understanding, and apply their learning in new situations and contexts. It is critical that the teacher verify student understanding during this stage.

5. **Evaluate**—The Evaluate phase is a formal assessment at the end of the cycle and contains performance assessments and/or selected-response items. Throughout the learning experience, however, the ongoing process of informal evaluation allows the teacher to determine whether the learner has reached the desired level of understanding of the key ideas and concepts.

If assessments of the student's progress indicate he or she has not mastered the learning, the teacher should re-enter the student at the appropriate point in the instructional model. Reiterate connections between past and present learning covered in the engagement phase. Use different materials to reinforce concepts, processes, and skills investigated during the exploration phase. Provide additional examples to allow extended time during the explanation phase to facilitate the student's understanding of the key ideas and concepts. Guided-practice activities may need further teacher support to connect, extend, and transfer learning to new situations; you may also need to provide increased feedback.

Table 5.1 (page 100) shows a 5E lesson plan template to help you plan lessons (also found in appendix C, page 196).

Table 5.1: A 5E Lesson Plan Template

Learning Phase	Developmental Progression	Type of Discourse	Activity Description	Facilitation Questions
Engage	How does this phase stimulate curiosity? How does this phase activate prior knowledge? What accommodations could I include in this phase to make learning more accessible? What questions might students raise?	Student–Student Student–Teacher Teacher–Student		
Explore	What concept(s) will students explore? What new vocabulary will students need for this phase of the lesson? What accommodations could I include in this phase to make learning more accessible?	Student–Student Student–Teacher Teacher–Student		
Explain	What connections are essential for the student to understand? What new vocabulary is introduced in this phase? What algorithms (computational procedures) are connected to the concept? What accommodations could I include in this phase to make learning more accessible?	Student–Student Student–Teacher Teacher–Student		
Elaborate	How is the new concept applied or extended? How will I encourage the use of vocabulary? What concepts and processes must students understand to be successful with this phase of the lesson? How (if at all) must the algorithms be applied? What accommodations could I include in this phase to make learning more accessible?	Student–Student Student–Teacher Teacher–Student		
Evaluate	What concept(s) will I assess? What additional skills must students have to complete this phase successfully? What accommodations could I include in this phase to make learning more accessible?	Student–Student Student–Teacher Teacher–Student		

You can also use a weekly checklist, such as the one in table 5.2, to verify that you've addressed each of Gardner's intelligences as discussed in chapter 4 in each learning phase.

Making Math Accessible to Students With Special Needs examines two mathematics lessons. In this chapter, we will examine a lesson on fractional parts and show how its approach meets the needs of students with special needs. In chapter 6, we will examine a traditional textbook lesson and show how to adapt it.

Table 5.2: Multiple Intelligences and the Phases of the 5E Lesson

	Engage	Explore	Explain	Elaborate	Evaluate
Linguistic (using words): Listening, speaking, writing, explaining					
Logical/mathematical (using numbers or logic): Problem solving, classifying, categorizing, defining relationships, questioning					
Visual/spatial (using pictures): Creating charts, graphs, organizers, sketching, using manipulatives, interpreting visual images					
Musical (using music): Creating songs for mathematical procedures, using sounds, rhythms, and patterns					
Intrapersonal (self-reflection): Journaling, evaluating thinking patterns, reasoning with themselves					
Interpersonal (using social experiences): Working in cooperative groups, problem solving with partners, teaching, creating mathematical problems for partner solving					
Bodily/kinesthetic (physical): Drilling using ball exercises, using manipulatives, physically creating shapes and constructs, doing physical experiments to develop mathematical relationships					
Naturalist (nature loving): Developing mathematical relationships using the natural world, classifying, categorizing					

A 5E Lesson on Equivalent Fractions

Figure 5.1 (page 102) summarizes the objective, materials, and preparation for our sample lesson on equivalent fractions. See appendix B (page 153) for reproducibles to use with students for this lesson.

(Teacher note: Keep in mind the types of disabilities in your classroom. Using explicit instructions and scaffolding the activities, questions, and features of each phase will allow your students with disabilities to successfully participate in this lesson.)

The important thing is not to stop questioning. Curiosity has its own reason for existing.

—Albert Einstein

Objective: Use appropriate language to describe part of a set, and use concrete models to represent and name fractional parts of a set.

Advanced preparation

☐ Prepare Fraction Circles set and Fraction Match Cards. Cut out circles.

For each student

☐ Journal

☐ Multiplication Chart (page 162)

☐ Scissors

☐ Vocabulary Organizer: Equivalent Fractions (page 163)

☐ Performance Assessment (page 168)

☐ Pattern blocks

For each pair of students

☐ Set Model Mats (pages 154–158), one set

☐ 18 counters (such as beans or centimeter cubes)

☐ Fraction Circles (pages 159–161), one set

☐ Fraction Match Cards (pages 164–167), copied on card stock and cut out

For each group of four students

☐ 15 circles cut from colored paper

☐ 5 sheets of manila paper

☐ Glue

Figure 5.1: Sample 5E lesson on equivalent fractions.

Engage Phase

1. Distribute fifteen colored paper circles and five sheets of manila paper to each group of four students.

2. Prompt the students to pretend that each colored paper circle represents a whole pizza. Prompt the students to divide one colored paper pizza so that each member of the group gets an equal share of the pizza.

3. Prompt the students to record their solution by gluing the pieces of pizza on a piece of manila paper.

Facilitation Questions

How did you make sure that each group member got an equal share of the pizza?
Possible average student response: We made sure that each person got the same size piece.
Possible struggling student response: Each group member received the same number of pieces of pizza.

State the difference between an equal share of something and the same number of pieces.

Were all of the pieces of pizza the same size?

When you compared the pieces of pizza that you received with the pieces that each of the other group members received, what did you notice? Were the pieces equivalent?

How would you describe the amount of pizza that each group member received?
Possible average student response: Each group member received one out of four equal pieces of the pizza.
Possible struggling student response: Each group member received some pizza.

What part of the whole pizza did each person receive?

Use numbers to describe the amount of pizza that each group member received.

How does the amount of pizza that each group member received compare to the total amount of pizza?

4. Prompt the students to divide two colored paper pizzas so that each member of the group gets an equal share.

5. Prompt the students to record their solution by gluing the pieces of pizza on a second piece of manila paper.

Facilitation Questions

How did you make sure that each group member got an equal share of the pizza?
Possible average student response: Each group member received an equal number of equal-sized pieces.
Possible struggling student response: Each group member received an equal amount of pizza.

continued ➡

How could you describe your process for comparing the amount of pizza that each group member received?

How would you describe the amount of pizza that each group member received?

Possible average student response: Each group member received half of a pizza.

Possible struggling student response: Each group member received one piece of pizza.

What portion of the pizza are you referring to when you say "one piece"?

How could you use a fraction to describe the part of the whole pizza that each person received?

How does the amount of pizza that each group member received compare to the total amount of pizza?

6. Repeat steps 4 and 5 with three, four, and five colored paper pizzas.

Facilitation Questions

How does the amount of pizza that each group member received when you shared two pizzas compare with the amount of pizza that each group member received when you shared five pizzas?

Possible average student response: When we shared two pizzas, each group member received less pizza than when we shared five pizzas.

Possible struggling student response: Each group member received the same amount of pizza.

What do you mean by same amount?

How could you describe the total amount of pizza that each group member received when you shared one pizza?

How could you describe the total amount of pizza that each group member received when you shared five pizzas?

What circumstances allowed each group member to receive at least one whole pizza?

Possible average student response: Each group member received at least one whole pizza when we shared four or more pizzas.

Possible struggling student response: When we cut the pizzas into a lot of parts, each group member received more pizza.

How can you describe the pieces of pizza that each group member received when you shared two pizzas?

How can you describe the pieces of pizza that each group member received when you shared three pizzas?

Was it easier to share two pizzas or to share three pizzas? Why or why not?

Possible average student response: It was easier to share two pizzas because all we had to do was cut each pizza in half, and we got four equal-sized pieces. When we shared three pizzas, we had to cut each pizza into more equal-sized parts in order to share it fairly.

Possible struggling student response: Sharing three pizzas gave us more pizza.

How can you describe the pieces of pizza that each group member received when you shared two pizzas?

How can you describe the pieces of pizza that each group member received when you shared three pizzas?

Task 5.1

Complete each section of table 5.3 for the Engage phase as directed. Compare your responses to those on page 148.

Table 5.3: Debriefing the Engage Phase of a 5E Lesson

Explain the Developmental Progression	Check the Type(s) of Discourse Used	Describe the Activity	Create Questions That Would Facilitate Sense-Making
How does this phase stimulate curiosity?	Student–Student Student–Teacher Teacher–Student		
How does this phase activate prior knowledge?			
What questions might students raise?			
What accommodations could be included in this phase to make learning more accessible?			

Reflection 5.1

Please respond to the following question. Write from your heart, your beliefs, and your past experience. Then compare your response to that on page 149.

What are some additional activities you could use in this phase of the lesson to draw on students' prior knowledge?

Explore Phase

1. Distribute one set of the Set Model Mats to each pair of students.

Facilitation Questions

How can you describe the Set Model Mats?
Possible average student response: The Set Model Mats are rectangles divided into equal parts, and the parts are labeled with fractions.
Possible struggling student response: The Set Model Mats have numbers on them.

What else do you notice about the Set Model Mats?

In what ways are the Set Model Mats similar?
Possible average student response: The Set Model Mats are all rectangles divided into equal parts.
Possible struggling student response: They all have parts.

How can you describe the parts of each rectangle?

How does one part of each rectangle compare to the other parts of the same rectangle?

In what ways are the Set Model Mats *different*?
Possible average student response: The Set Model Mats are divided into different numbers of equal parts, and the parts on each of the rectangles are different sizes.
Possible struggling student response: The parts of the rectangles are different.

How do the parts on the Set Model Mat: Halves compare to the parts on the Set Model Mat: Fourths?

---

2. Distribute twelve counters (such as beans or centimeter cubes) to each pair of students.

3. Prompt the students to divide the counters evenly between the parts on the Set Model Mat: Halves.

4. Prompt the students to discuss their findings with their partners and record their conclusions.

5. Prompt the students to repeat steps 3 and 4 for each Set Model Mat.

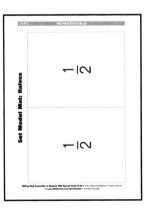

Facilitation Questions

Were you able to divide the twelve counters equally on all of the Set Model Mats?

What are some of the conclusions that you recorded about the models?

Possible average student response: We were able to divide the set of twelve counters equally on each of the Set Model Mats. We could see that the set of counters was divided into equal groups.

Possible struggling student response: One rectangle had three counters.

How does the number of counters in each part of the Set Model Mat: Halves compare to the number of counters in each part of the Set Model Mat: Fourths?

How many counters were placed in each part of the Set Model Mat: Halves?

Possible average student response: Six.

Possible struggling student response: Twelve.

Tell me how your model shows twelve counters in each part.

What is the relationship between $\frac{1}{12}$ and $\frac{1}{2}$?

Possible average student response: $\frac{6}{12} = \frac{1}{2}$.

Possible struggling student response: There are six in one and twelve in two.

How could you use fractions to describe your model?

(Teacher note: Repeat facilitation questions for Thirds, Fourths, Sixths, and Twelfths.)

6. Record the equivalent fractions on a board, chart paper, or overhead.

7. Distribute six more counters to each pair of students.

8. Prompt the students to repeat steps 3–5 with eighteen counters. Prompt the students to discuss their findings with their partner and record their conclusions.

Facilitation Questions

Were you able to divide the eighteen counters equally on each Set Model Mat?

Possible average student response: No.
Possible struggling student response: Yes.

On which Set Model Mats was it impossible to divide the counters equally?

Possible average student response: Set Model Mat: Fourths and Set Model Mat: Twelfths.
Possible struggling student response: Set Model Mat: Thirds

How many counters are in each part of your Thirds mat?

How many total counters are on your Thirds mat?

What are some of the conclusions that you recorded about these models?

Possible average student response: If the number of parts on the Set Model Mat was a factor of 18, we could divide the counters equally on that mat.
Possible struggling student response: It didn't work on some mats.

What makes you say that it didn't work on some mats?

What is the relationship between 2 and 18?

Possible average student response: Two times 9 is equal to 18.
Possible struggling student response: 2 and 18 are both even numbers.

What is the relationship between 2 and 18 on your Set Model Mat: Halves?

How many counters were placed in each part of the Set Model Mat: Halves?

What is the relationship between $\frac{9}{18}$ and $\frac{1}{2}$?

Possible average student response: $\frac{9}{18} = \frac{1}{2}$.
Possible struggling student response: There is nine in one and eighteen in two.

How could you use fractions to describe your model?

(Teacher note: Repeat facilitation questions for Thirds and Sixths.)

9. Record the equivalent fractions on a board, chart paper, or overhead.

Task 5.2

Complete each section of table 5.4 for the Explore phase as directed. Compare your responses to those on page 149.

Table 5.4: Debriefing the Explore Phase of a 5E Lesson

Explain the Developmental Progression	Check the Type(s) of Discourse Used	Describe the Activity	Create Questions That Would Facilitate Sense-Making
What concepts does this phase explore? **What vocabulary will students need?** **What accommodations could be included in this phase to make learning more accessible?**	Student–Student Student–Teacher Teacher–Student		

Reflection 5.2

Please respond to the following question. Write from your heart, your beliefs, and your past experience. Then compare your response to that on page 149.

What are some additional activities that could be used in this phase of the lesson that would assist students in developing the relationship _____ out of _____ ?

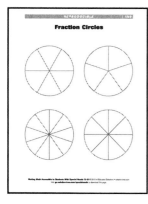

Explain Phase

1. Distribute one set of Fraction Circles to each pair of students.

2. Prompt the students to use the Fraction Circles to model $\frac{1}{2}$.

3. Prompt the students to use the Fraction Circles to find all possible representations of fractions equivalent to $\frac{1}{2}$.

Facilitation Questions

What patterns are created by the numerators and denominators of the fractions that are equivalent to $\frac{1}{2}$?

Possible average student response: The numerator of each fraction is half of the denominator. The denominator of each fraction is two times the numerator.

Possible struggling student response: The denominators are even.

What else do you notice about the patterns created by the numerator and denominator of the fractions?

What could you multiply each of the numerators by in order to get the denominator?

What could you divide each of the denominators by in order to get the numerator?

---

4. Record the following expression on a board, chart paper, or overhead (see fig. 5.2).

$$\frac{1 \times \square}{2 \times \square} = \frac{3}{6}$$

Figure 5.2: Fraction problem.

Facilitation Questions

Is $\frac{1}{2}$ equivalent to $\frac{3}{6}$? How do you know?

Possible average student response: Yes. The models of $\frac{1}{2}$ and $\frac{3}{6}$ represent the same fractional part of one whole.

Possible struggling student response: No. The numbers are not the same.

What else do you notice about the size of a fraction circle model representing $\frac{1}{2}$ compared with the size of a fraction circle model representing $\frac{3}{6}$?

continued ➡

> What number could we place in each blank to make the expression true?
>   *Possible average student response: Three.*
>   *Possible struggling student response: Six.*
>
> What factor could you multiply by one to equal three? What factor could you multiply by two to equal six?

5. Record the following expression on a board, chart paper, or overhead (fig. 5.3).

$$\frac{6 \times \square}{12 \times \square} = \frac{1}{2}$$

Figure 5.3: Fraction problem, continued.

Facilitation Questions

Is $\frac{6}{12}$ equivalent to $\frac{1}{2}$? How do you know?
  Possible average student response: Yes. The models of $\frac{6}{12}$ and $\frac{1}{2}$ represent the same fractional part of one whole.
  Possible struggling student response: No. The numbers are not the same.

What else do you know about how the size of a fraction circle model representing $\frac{1}{2}$ compares with the size of a fraction circle model representing $\frac{3}{6}$?

What number could we place in each blank to make the expression true?
  Possible average student response: Six.
  Possible struggling student response: Two?

6. Distribute the Multiplication Chart and pair of scissors to each student.

7. Prompt the students to cut along the dotted lines of each horizontal row of the multiplication chart to create strips of multiples.

8. Prompt the students to take the strip that starts with the number 1 and place it directly on top of the strip that starts with the number 2 (fig. 5.4).

1	2	3	4	5	6	7	8	9	10	11	12
2	4	6	8	10	12	14	16	18	20	22	24

Figure 5.4: Number strip.

Facilitation Questions

If we view each vertical pair of numbers as a fraction, what fractions are created that were on our list of equivalent fractions?

Possible average student response: $\frac{1}{2}, \frac{3}{6}, \frac{6}{12}, \frac{9}{18}$.

Possible struggling student response: The top row counts by ones, and the bottom row skip-counts by two.

What do the top row and bottom row represent?

What conclusions can we draw about the other fractions created by the number strips?

Possible average student response: The fractions are equivalent to $\frac{1}{2}$.

Possible struggling student response: The fractions get bigger.

How are the fractions represented in the circle models and the number strips similar/different?

---

9. Repeat steps 2–8 and facilitation questions for other unit fractions such as $\frac{1}{4}$ and $\frac{1}{3}$.

10. Prompt the students to complete the Vocabulary Organizer reproducible (see fig. 5.5, page 114).

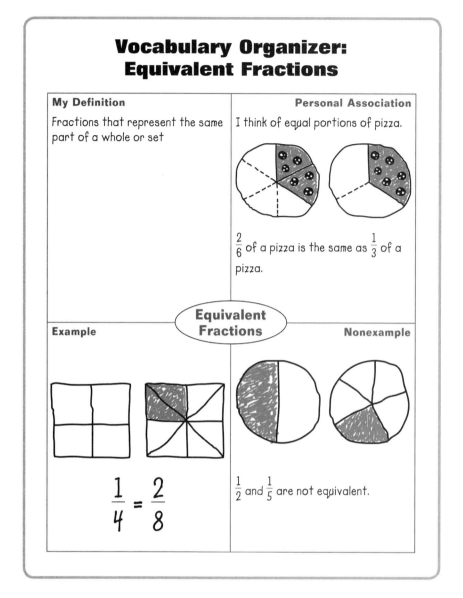

Figure 5.5: Sample vocabulary development for lesson on fractions.

The Explain phase explicitly clarifies important mathematical connections. Teachers use questioning strategies to lead student discussion of information discovered during the Explore phase. Teachers introduce new terms and explanations at appropriate times during the discussion.

Task 5.3

Complete each section of table 5.5 for the Explain phase as directed. Compare your responses to those on page 149.

Table 5.5: Debriefing the Explain Phase of a 5E Lesson

Explain the Developmental Progression	Check the Type(s) of Discourse Used	Describe the Activity	Create Questions That Would Facilitate Sense-Making
What connections are essential for the student to understand?	Student–Student Student–Teacher Teacher–Student		
What new vocabulary is introduced?			
What algorithms are connected to the concept?			
What accommodations could be included in this phase to make learning more accessible?			

Elaborate Phase

1. Distribute one set of the Fraction Match Cards to each pair of students.

2. Prompt the students to match each fraction card with the equivalent area model card, set model card, and number line card.

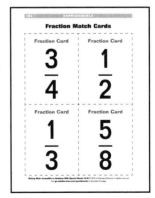

Facilitation Questions

How does the total number of parts in each area model card compare to the denominator of the equivalent fraction on the fraction card?

Possible average student response: The total number of parts in each model is twice the denominator.

Possible struggling student response: The total number of parts in each model is bigger than the denominator of the fraction.

What is another way to describe how the total number of parts in each area model card compares to the denominator of the equivalent fraction on the fraction card?

Is there a number that we can multiply or divide by the number of parts in each area model to equal the number in the denominator of the equivalent fraction?

How can we describe the relationship between the total number of objects in each set model card and the denominator of the equivalent fraction on the fraction card?

Possible average student response: The total number of objects is three times the denominator.

Possible struggling student response: The total number of parts in each model is bigger than the denominator of the fraction.

What is another way we could describe the relationship between the total number of objects in each set model card and the denominator of the equivalent fraction on the fraction card?

Is there a number that we can multiply or divide by the number of objects in each set model to equal the number in the denominator of the equivalent fraction?

What strategy did you use to match a number line card with its equivalent fraction card?

Possible average student response: We determined how many equal parts each number line was divided into between 0 and 1. Then we determined the fractional part of the whole represented by the distance from 0 to point A.

Possible struggling student response: I found a card that put the fraction close to the middle.

What do you mean when you say "close to the middle"?

What were you thinking that made you decide to find a card with a point "close to the middle"?

Task 5.4

Complete each section of table 5.6 for the Elaborate phase as directed. Compare your responses to those on page 150.

Table 5.6: Debriefing the Elaborate Phase of a 5E Lesson

Explain the Developmental Progression	Check the Type(s) of Discourse Used	Describe the Activity	Create Questions That Would Facilitate Sense-Making
How is the new concept applied or extended?	Student–Student Student–Teacher Teacher–Student		
How is the use of vocabulary encouraged?			
What understanding must the student have to be successful with this phase of the lesson?			
How (if at all) must the algorithms be applied?			
What accommodations could be included in this phase to make learning more accessible?			

Reflection 5.3

Please respond to the following question. Write from your heart, your beliefs, and your past experience. Then compare your response to that on page 150.

What are some additional activities you could use in this phase of the lesson to assist students in understanding the relationship of the concrete representation to the number sentence?

Evaluate Phase

1. Distribute the Performance Assessment and a set of pattern blocks to each student.

2. Prompt the students to use the pattern blocks to create a model of the fraction $\frac{1}{3}$. Say,

   If each hexagon has a value equal to 1, use pattern blocks to create a fraction model of $\frac{1}{3}$. Create a model of a fraction that is equivalent to $\frac{1}{3}$. Draw a sketch of your models. Explain your thinking.

Task 5.5

Complete each section of table 5.7 for the Evaluate phase as directed. Compare your responses to those on page 150.

Table 5.7: Debriefing the Evaluate Phase of a 5E Lesson

Explain the Developmental Progression	Check the Type(s) of Discourse Used	Describe the Activity	Create Questions That Would Facilitate Sense-Making
What concepts are addressed in this phase?	Student–Student Student–Teacher Teacher–Student		
What additional skills must the students have to successfully complete this phase?			
What accommodations could be included in this phase to make learning more accessible?			

Reflection 5.4

Please respond to the following questions. Write from your heart, your beliefs, and your past experience. Then compare your responses to those on page 151.

Consider how our four students—Rafael, Andy, Rachelle, and Zack—could benefit from the 5E instructional model.

Rafael has been diagnosed as autistic. He gets along well with classmates. Rafael dislikes math and occasionally makes loud unexpected comments when frustrated. He sometimes takes out his visual dictionary and reads instead of doing his math.

1. *What visual dictionary entry could you create to support Rafael?*

Andy is a student with a learning disability in reading who is learning in an inclusive classroom. He is not disruptive. He is actually rather passive in class, and his former teachers say that he has the ability but lacks motivation. Occasionally he engages other students in off-task behavior. Andy rarely does his homework and either asks questions or sits passively when it's time to do independent work.

2. *How might recording text read aloud help Andy during this lesson?*

Rachelle works very hard in class but doesn't seem to "get it" when concepts are integrated together. She is polite and raises her hand for assistance. Her functional skill level in mathematics is about two years behind grade level. She has been placed in a general education mathematics class. She seems to know something one day but not the next.

3. *How might the follow-up questions help Rachelle?*

Zack is eligible for special education services in the category of emotional disturbance. He often sits by himself and makes demeaning remarks about others in the room. He is often staring out of the window or drawing pictures. He does some classwork that shows a good level of understanding. Most students avoid him.

4. *How might asking Zack to create a poster that summarizes the lesson help him?*

Big
Ideas of
Chapter 5

- The 5E instructional model has unique benefits for all students, particularly students with special needs. The five phases of the 5E model are:

  1. Engage—Designed to interest students in the problem and to make connections between past and present learning.

  2. Explore—Designed to provide the opportunity for students to become directly involved with the key concepts with the teacher observing and listening to students as they interact with each other.

  3. Explain—Designed for the teacher to act as a facilitator to formalize understanding, correct any misconceptions, and provide further meaning or information.

  4. Elaborate—Designed to allow students to extend and expand what they have learned in the first three phases.

  5. Evaluate—Designed to allow the teacher to determine whether the learner has reached the desired level of understanding of the key ideas and concepts.

Chapter 6

Creating and Adapting Lessons for High-Quality Instruction

The only limit to our realization of tomorrow will be our doubts of today.

—Franklin D. Roosevelt

Traditional textbook lessons present several concerns. The lesson format generally lends itself to teacher-centered instruction instead of student-centered instruction. The content of standard textbook lessons rarely includes examples and problems with the cognitive rigor necessary to prepare students for success—whether success is measured by standardized tests or readiness for post–high school education. Such lessons seldom include strategies for building common background, developing vocabulary, providing comprehensibility, and solving authentic problems in an atmosphere ripe for interaction. Therefore, teachers often face the challenge of creating lessons or adapting textbook lessons to meet the needs of students with special needs. Adapting a textbook lesson to create high-quality instruction involves a few subtle but important changes. Let's take a look at a typical textbook lesson (see fig. 6.1, pages 122–123).

Multiplication

Lesson objective: To explore multiplication

Introduction

James is planting bean plants in his garden. He will plant 4 bean plants in each row. If there are 3 rows in his garden, how many bean plants will James need?

Lesson

Use counters to create **equal groups**.	Use **repeated addition**.
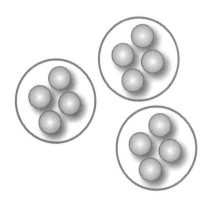	$4 + 4 + 4 = 12$
Build an **array**. 4 columns 3 rows 3 rows of 4 squares equals 12 squares.	Write a **multiplication sentence**. $3 \times 4 = 12$ 3 and 4 are factors. 12 is the product.

Check

Copy and complete.

1. 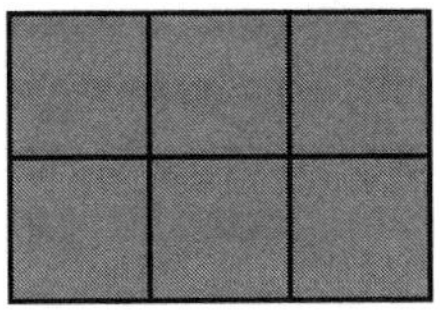 a. $\square + \square = \square$

   b. $\square \times \square = \square$

2. 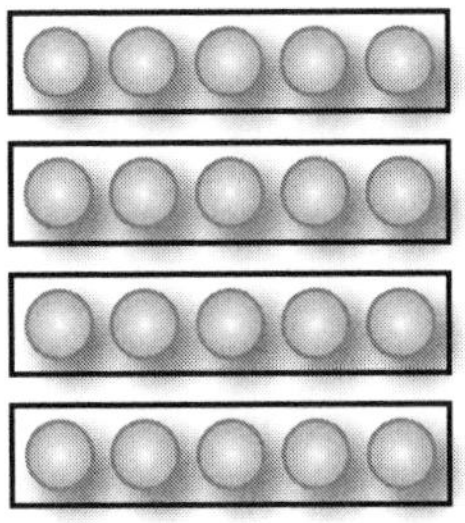 a. $\square + \square = \square$

   b. $\square \times \square = \square$

3. $2 \times 4 = 8$

   a. What are the factors in this number sentence?

   b. Which number in the number sentence is the product?

   c. Draw an array for this number sentence.

Practice

Write a multiplication sentence and draw a picture.

4. 5 groups of 2

5. 6 groups of 3

6. 4 groups of 1

Figure 6.1: Sample traditional textbook lesson.

Making a few significant additions and changing the lesson from direct instruction to inquiry-based instruction will provide critical components of high-quality instruction. To adapt a lesson, take the following steps.

1. Answer the following questions for yourself: What standards does the lesson address? What needs to be added to the lesson to reflect the depth and complexity of the standards? What outcome do you want?

2. Tie the mathematical concepts and skills to real-life experiences and problems.

3. Provide opportunities for student-to-student discourse. Use think-pair-share or any problem-solving activity. Say:

   - *Take one minute to develop your own thoughts and ideas on what might be a good strategy for solving the problem, or see if you can give a good solution.*

   - *Discuss your ideas with your partner.*

   - *Now share your idea with the rest of the class* [or *with your team of four*].

4. Provide opportunities for students to make conjectures from patterns or sets of examples and nonexamples.

5. Use teacher-generated and student-generated facilitation questions to make meaning of the mathematics.

6. Use and ensure that students use multiple representations to describe mathematical concepts: concrete models, pictures, verbal descriptions, tables, graphs, diagrams, equations, examples, and nonexamples.

7. Bridge from the concrete to the pictorial to the abstract by making the connections explicitly and giving students the opportunity to also make the connections. The concrete model should be on the student's desk while the student is creating the pictorial model. The pictorial model should be on the student's desk when the student is creating the abstract (mathematical or algorithmic) model.

8. Provide worksheets with ample space to show work, answers, and rationales.

9. Ask (Van de Walle, 2001, p. 437):

   - *How did you solve the problem?*

- *Why did you solve it this way?*

- *Why do you think your solution is correct and makes sense?*

Creating a High-Quality Lesson

When creating a new lesson, start by using the 5E Lesson Plan Template and/or the 5E Lesson Plan Short Form (appendix C, pages 196–198) to generate ideas, describe activities, and script facilitation questions. The rest of this chapter explores a lesson on multiplication that follows the 5E model. Table 6.1 shows the lesson objectives and materials.

Table 6.1: 5E Lesson on Multiplication

Lesson Objectives/Standards Addressed	
Learn and apply multiplication facts through 12 × 12 using concrete models and objects.	
Model factors and products using arrays and area models.	
Use multiplication to solve problems involving whole numbers.	
Identify common factors of a set of whole numbers.	
Advanced Preparation	
Apple Counters (cut apart)	
Product Finders transparency strips (cut apart)	
Materials	
Garden Problem (page 169)	**For each student**
Window Pane Problem-Solving Cards (pages 170–175)	3 popsicle sticks
	Modeling clay
Station 1	Window Pane Problem-Solving Recording Sheets (pages 176–178)
Calendar (page 179)	Multiplication Chart (page 162)
40 counters (such as beans, two-color counters, or centimeter cubes)	Product Finders transparency strips (1 of each pattern) (page 181)
Station 2	Vocabulary Organizer: Factor (page 182)
6 portion cups	Vocabulary Organizer: Product (page 183)
40 beans	The Product Is . . . reproducibles (pages 184–187)
Station 3	
40 square tiles	40 square tiles
Station 4	Square-Inch Grid Paper (as needed) (page 188)
6 string loops	Square-Centimeter Grid Paper (as needed) (page 189)
40 counters (such as beans, two-color counters, or centimeter cubes)	
Station 5	Performance Assessment (page 190)
40 unifix cubes	Base-10 blocks (tens and ones)
Station 6	
Apple Counters (page 180)	
Multiplication Chart (page 162)	
Chart paper	

Engage Phase

1. Display the Garden Problem on an overhead projector.

2. Distribute three popsicle sticks and a portion of clay to each student.

3. Prompt the students to build a model of the problem situation.

Facilitation Questions

What could the popsicle sticks represent in the story? Why?
Possible average student response: The rows in the garden, because there are three popsicle sticks, and the story says that there are three rows of beans.
Possible struggling student response: The bean plants.

What words in the story made you think that the popsicle sticks are the best way to represent the bean plants?

What could the small balls of clay represent in the story?
Possible average student response: The bean plants.
Possible struggling student response: The rows of bean plants.

What words in the story made you think that the clay is the best way to represent the rows of bean plants?

How many popsicle sticks did you use? Why?
Possible average student response: I used three because the popsicle sticks represent rows, and the problem states that James is planting three rows of bean plants.
Possible struggling student response: I used four because the number 4 is in the problem.

What do the balls of clay represent in the problem?

What does the number 4 describe in the problem?

How many balls of clay do we need to place on each popsicle stick? Why?
Possible average student response: We need four because the balls of clay represent the bean plants, and the problem states that James planted four bean plants in each row.
Possible struggling student response: We need three because the number 3 is in the problem.

What do the popsicle sticks represent in the problem?

What does the number 3 describe in the problem?

> How did you determine the total number of bean plants needed to fill three rows?
>   *Possible average student response: I counted the number of balls of clay on all of the popsicle sticks. I counted by 4 three times. I added 4 + 4 + 4.*
>   *Possible struggling student response: I counted. I added.*
>
> Can you give me an example of how you counted?
>
> Can you give me an example of how you added?

Explore Phase

1. Place a Window Pane Problem-Solving Card and the appropriate manipulatives in six different stations around the classroom (see fig. 6.2).

Station 1	Calendar and 40 counters
Station 2	6 portion cups and 40 beans
Station 3	40 square tiles
Station 4	6 string loops and 40 counters
Station 5	40 unifix cubes
Station 6	Apple Counters, Multiplication Chart, and chart paper

Figure 6.2: Window Pane Problem-Solving Card stations.

2. Divide the students into groups of three or four.

3. Distribute the Window Pane Problem-Solving Recording Sheets to each student.

4. Prompt the students to rotate through each station and use the manipulatives there to represent each problem situation.

5. Prompt the students to record their work on the Window Pane Problem-Solving Recording Sheets.

6. Assign each group one of the Window Pane Problem-Solving Cards.

7. Prompt the students to display their solutions from the Window Pane Problem-Solving Recording Sheets on chart paper.

   Note: To avoid students writing the entire problem, they could glue or tape the Window Pane Problem-Solving Card in the problem section of their chart paper.

8. Prompt the students to display the piece of chart paper containing their solutions.

Facilitation Questions

What do you understand about the problem?
Possible average student response (Station 1): Millie's vacation was four weeks long, and there are seven days in a week.
Possible struggling student response (Station 1): Millie went on vacation for seven days.

How many weeks was Millie on vacation?

What is the problem prompting you to determine?
Possible average student response (Station 2): The problem is prompting me to determine the total number of model cars that the boys purchased.
Possible struggling student response (Station 2): The problem is prompting me to determine the number of boys that purchased model cars.

What in the problem makes you say that the problem is prompting you determine the number of boys that purchased model cars?

What operation is implied by the problem?
Possible average student response (Station 3): The problem implies the use of addition, because I could add six fives to determine the total number of desks in Mrs. Milburn's arrangement.
Possible struggling student response (Station 3): The problem implies the use of addition because I could add 6 and 5 to determine the total number of desks in Mrs. Milburn's arrangement.

How many desks are in each row?

How many rows are in Mrs. Milburn's arrangement?

(Teacher note: Repeat facilitation questions as needed for other stations.)

Explain Phase

1. Explain to students that multiplication is a process for combining same-size groups.

2. For each Window-Pane Problem Solving Card, ask facilitation questions.

Facilitation Questions

How many times was _____ added?
  Possible average student response (Station 1): The number 7 was added four times.
  Possible struggling student response (Station 1): The number 7 was added seven times.

What makes you say that?

How are groups represented in this problem?
  Possible average student response (Station 4): The fishbowls represent the groups.
  Possible struggling student response (Station 4): The fish represent the groups.

Can you draw a picture of the groups?

How many groups are represented?
  Possible average student response (Station 5): Four groups are represented.
  Possible struggling student response (Station 5): Nine groups are represented.

How do you know that?

How can we represent the situation as repeated addition?
  Possible average student response (Station 6): We could represent this problem as 3 + 3 + 3 + 3, because in the problem that we wrote, there are four baskets with three apples in each basket.
  Possible struggling student response (Station 6): We could represent this problem as 4 + 3, because in the problem that we wrote, there are four baskets and three apples.

How many apples are in each basket?

What is the problem prompting you to determine?

What do we call the numbers that are added together?
  Possible average student response: Addends.
  Possible struggling student response: Sum.

Define *addend*. Define *sum*.

What do we call the result of an addition problem situation?
  Possible average student response: Sum.
  Possible struggling student response: Difference.

Define *sum*. Define *difference*.

(Teacher note: Repeat facilitation questions as needed for other stations.)

3. Explain to the students that we can use multiplication to represent $7 + 7 + 7 = 21$ as $7 \times 3 = 21$.

4. Explain to the students that the numbers being multiplied are called *factors*.

5. Explain to the students that the result of a multiplication problem is called the *product*.

6. For each Window Pane Problem-Solving Card, prompt the students to identify the factors and the product.

7. Distribute a Multiplication Chart to each student, and display the Multiplication Chart on the overhead.

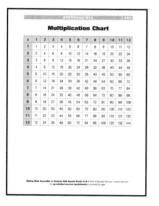

Facilitation Questions

Which numbers on the Multiplication Chart represent factors?
Possible average student response: The numbers in the shaded row and column represent factors.
Possible struggling student response: All of the numbers on the chart.

Give me an example of a factor. How does your example align with your previous answer?

Which numbers on the Multiplication Chart represent products?
Possible average student response: The numbers that are not in the shaded row and column are products.
Possible struggling student response: The shaded numbers.

What else do you know about products? What did you mean by that?

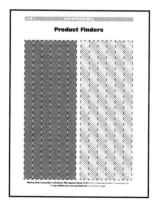

8. Distribute two Product Finders transparency strips (one of each type of shading) to each student.

9. Record the following problem on the board: $6 \times 4 = $ _____.

10. Prompt the students to place one Product Finders transparency strip on the row on the Multiplication Chart that starts with 6.

11. Prompt the students to place the remaining Product Finders transparency strip on the column on the Multiplication Chart that starts with 4 (see fig. 6.3).

x	1	2	3	4	5	6	7	8	9	10	11	12
1	1	2	3	4	5	6	7	8	9	10	11	12
2	2	4	6	8	10	12	14	16	18	20	22	24
3	3	6	9	12	15	18	21	24	27	30	33	36
4	4	8	12	16	20	24	27	32	36	40	44	48
5	5	10	15	20	25	30	35	40	45	50	55	60
6	6	12	18	24	30	36	42	48	54	60	66	72
7	7	14	21	28	35	42	49	56	63	70	77	84
8	8	16	24	32	40	48	56	64	72	80	88	96
9	9	18	27	36	45	54	63	72	81	90	99	108
10	10	20	30	40	50	60	70	80	90	100	110	120
11	11	22	33	44	55	66	77	88	99	110	121	132
12	12	24	36	48	60	72	84	96	108	120	132	144

Figure 6.3: Using Product Finders.

Facilitation Questions

Why do you think we chose to place one of the Product Finders on the row that begins with 6 and the other Product Finder on the column that begins with 4?
 Possible average student response: Because 6 and 4 are the factors in the problem.
 Possible struggling student response: Because those are the numbers in the problem.

What are you referring to when you say "the numbers in the problem"?

Define *factor.*

What number appears where the two Product Finders intersect?
 Possible average student response: 24.
 Possible struggling student response: 20.

Show me where the "6" row and the "4" column intersect.

What word would you use to describe the number 24?
 Possible average student response: Product.
 Possible struggling student response: Sum.

Define *product.* Define *sum.*

continued ➡

> Explain how you could use the Multiplication Chart and the Product Finders transparency strips to find the product of 12 × 11.
>
> *Possible average student response: I would place one Product Finders strip on the row that begins with 12 and the other Product Finders strip on the column that begins with 11. The product of 12 × 11 will appear where the two Product Finders strips intersect.*
>
> *Possible struggling student response: I would put the strips on the two numbers and find the answer.*
>
> Show me exactly how you would place the Product Finders transparency strips on the Multiplication Chart.
>
> Explain how you would use the Product Finders transparency strips and the Multiplication Chart to find two factors of 48.
>
> *Possible average student response: I would place the Product Finders strips so that they intersect at the number 48 on the Multiplication Chart. Then I would look to see which row and column the Product Finders strips were placed upon to determine the factors.*
>
> *Possible struggling student response: I would put the Product Finders strips on 48 and look for the other numbers.*
>
> What do you mean by "look for the other numbers"?
>
> Can you demonstrate your strategy for finding two factors of 48?

12. Prompt the students to use the Product Finders and the Multiplication Chart to explore other factors and products.

13. Distribute the Vocabulary Organizers for *factor* and *product* to each student.

14. Prompt the students to complete the Vocabulary Organizers.

Elaborate Phase

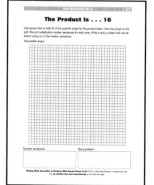

1. Distribute the The Product Is . . . reproducibles and forty square tiles to each student.

2. Prompt the students to use the square tiles to build all of the possible arrays for the given product.

3. Prompt the students to record the arrays on the grid of each reproducible.

Note: Some students may have difficulty drawing representations of the square tile arrays on the grids of the reproducibles. Square grid paper accommodates this need for children (see pages 188 and 189).

4. Prompt the students to record the multiplication number sentence that represents each of the arrays created.

5. Prompt the students to write a story problem that can be represented by one of the number sentences.

Facilitation Questions

What patterns do you notice in the arrays for each product?
  Possible average student response: The number of squares on each side of each array is the same as the factors for that product.
  Possible struggling student response: I don't know.

What do you observe about the length of each side of each array?

How can you use your Multiplication Chart to show how these numbers are related?

What patterns do you notice in the number sentences for each array?
  Possible average student response: The factors in the number sentences are the same as the lengths of the sides of the arrays.
  Possible struggling student response: The numbers are the same.

What do you mean when you say, "The numbers are the same"?

Evaluate Phase

1. Provide each student with a copy of the Performance Assessment reproducible. You may also wish to distribute the Problem-Solving Organizer from appendix C (page 194) to each student.

2. Prompt the students to use base-10 blocks to solve the problem, then record a picture to represent how they used the base-10 blocks to solve the problem.

3. Prompt the students to record the number sentence they used to solve the problem.

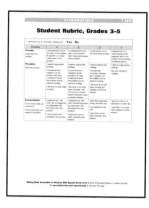

4. Prompt the students to explain their thinking.

5. A student rubric is provided in appendix C (page 193) to use when evaluating student work.

By adapting a more traditional instructional model to the 5E instructional model, a few significant changes or additions can yield a lesson that is inquiry-based with key elements of high-quality instruction.Begin by adapting or creating an activity to engage your students with the topic, writing facilitation questions using strategies from chapter 3 as a guide, and scripting anticipated student responses for your average and struggling students. Consider what adaptations you can incorporate in the initial design of the lesson and what supports you may need to add for all students to be successful.

Big
Ideas of
Chapter 6

- Traditional textbook lessons can be adapted to make instruction more accessible.

- Including elements of high-quality instruction in presentations of textbook lessons and in teacher-created lessons benefits all students.

Epilogue

Task E.1

Table E.1 contains effective, high-quality instructional strategies derived from some of the ideas discussed earlier in the book. Fill out the table to indicate which of these instructional strategies you currently use. Be sure to note what evidence you have that you're using the strategies. Answers will vary.

Table E.1: Evaluating Your Use of Instructional Strategies

Instructional Strategy	Used in Your Classroom?	Evidence
Use a problem-based approach to learning.		
Use learning by doing as an alternative to teacher-centered instruction.		
Use prior knowledge and experiences as a bridge to new learning.		
Plan lessons that emphasize higher-level and critical thinking skills.		
Plan lessons that address multiple intelligences.		
Plan tiered instruction.		
Use manipulatives and multiple representations to bridge from the concrete to the abstract.		
Use graphic representations to enhance student memory.		

continued ➡

Instructional Strategy	Used in Your Classroom?	Evidence
Use an advanced graphic organizer for new concepts and lessons.		
Develop students' self-control through cooperative learning activities and modeling.		
Use classwide peer tutoring.		
Praise efforts even if they lead to an incorrect solution.		
Encourage, praise, and help struggling students.		
Give positive comments about student questions.		
Use strategies that encourage students to ask questions.		
Use facilitation questions to help students solve problems rather than giving them the answers.		
Use wait time; pause for at least three seconds after asking a question and three seconds before responding.		
Post questions for students to ask themselves as they solve problems. (See appendix C, page 195.)		
Explicitly teach problem-solving strategies.		
Allow time for problem solving.		
Provide sample problems with detailed solutions for students to use as a guide when solving other problems.		
Use students' prior knowledge to create challenging word problems that students will enjoy solving.		
Reinforce visualization skills by guiding students in making mental pictures when applying problem-solving rules.		
Structure lessons to enable students to think aloud during problem solving.		
Use group problem solving to stimulate students in applying mathematical thinking skills.		
Give prompt feedback on performance.		
Refrain from giving graded feedback too early. Use written and verbal feedback to increase student understanding.		

Reflection E.1

Using table E.1, identify an instructional strategy for each of the four students with special needs that would help him or her access the curriculum. Then compare your responses to those on page 151.

Rafael has been diagnosed as autistic. He gets along well with classmates. Rafael dislikes math and occasionally makes loud unexpected comments when frustrated. He sometimes takes out his visual dictionary and reads instead of doing his math.

1. *What practice will best help Rafael to communicate his mathematical ability?*

Andy is a student with a learning disability in reading who is learning in an inclusive classroom. He is not disruptive. He is actually rather passive in class, and his former teachers say that he has the ability but lacks motivation. Occasionally he engages other students in off-task behavior. Andy rarely does his homework and either asks questions or sits passively when it's time to do independent work.

2. *What practice will best help Andy demonstrate his mathematics understanding?*

Rachelle works very hard in class but doesn't seem to "get it" when concepts are integrated together. She is polite and raises her hand for assistance. Her functional skill level in mathematics is about two years behind grade level. She has been placed in a general education mathematics class. She seems to know something one day but not the next.

3. *What practice will best help Rachelle develop a thorough, long-term understanding of the mathematics?*

Zack is eligible for special education services in the category of emotional disturbance. He often sits by himself and makes barely audible demeaning remarks about others in the room. He is often staring out of the window or drawing pictures. He does some classwork that shows a good level of understanding. Most students avoid him.

4. *What practice will best help Zack demonstrate his mathematics ability in an appropriate way?*

Reflection E.2

What is the first step you need to take in order to implement high-quality instruction for all students? What actions are you willing to implement over the next six weeks to improve the quality of instruction in your classroom? Answers will vary.

Task E.2

Please give a short response to each of the questions in table E.2. As you refine your high-quality instructional practices, reflect on these components at two additional times during the instructional year. Record the date of each reflection. Answers will vary.

Table E.2: Implementing High-Quality Instructional Practices

Practice	Reflection
How do I implement the federal and state legislation that governs instructional expectations for all students?	
How do I ensure that all students understand my belief that they can learn and that I hold high expectations for all students?	
How do I ensure that my students and I exist in a safe environment?	
What components of the 5E lesson model do I need to refine in my instruction?	
How do I initiate or improve cooperative learning strategies in my classroom?	
How do I improve the key and follow-up facilitation questions in my lessons?	

Practice	Reflection
How do I incorporate additional performance assessments in my classroom?	
How do I ensure that students in my classroom regularly create and use graphic organizers and multiple representations?	
How do I avoid engaging in learned helpfulness but remain responsive and supportive of my students?	
How do I improve my mathematical knowledge of teaching to increase my teaching proficiency?	

Responses to Tasks and Reflections

Reflection 1.1

1. Answers will vary.

2. Some students are cognitively incapable of learning enrolled grade-level mathematics with understanding, but this is a very small percent of the student population.

3. No Child Left Behind legislation requires schools to make enrolled grade-level mathematics accessible to 99 percent of students. It is estimated that 0.5 percent of students are cognitively incapable of accessing enrolled grade-level mathematics. Doubling that number gives us the 1 percent cap.

Reflection 1.2

1. Students with disabilities, English language learners, and students who are African American, Hispanic, or economically disadvantaged all scored lower than all students or white students.

2. Answers will vary.

3. Experience has taught us to look at previous grades when student performance doesn't meet expectations. Examining the foundation for mathematics in grades 3–5 is critical. Mathematics instruction in 3–5 must be changed in order for these groups to become successful.

Task 1.1

1. Answers will vary.

2. Three categories—learning disabilities, speech or language impairments, and other health impairments—make up over 70 percent of the students with special needs. The challenge lies in finding the strategies that work so that 99 percent of all students can access and become proficient at grade-level mathematics.

Reflection 1.3

1. It is impossible to predict what any student is capable of accomplishing. Many world leaders were struggling students, for example, Albert Einstein, John F. Kennedy, and Winston Churchill.

2. It is critical to give every student the opportunity to master mathematics. Our instructional decisions can facilitate or hinder this process. Offering those opportunities through instructional best practices is key.

3. As more students with special needs are placed in general education classes, instruction must change to meet these needs.

Task 1.2

Answers will vary.

Reflection 2.1

1. A supportive classroom environment is characterized by high expectations and support for all students. It is an environment in which students feel safe to take risks and ask for and give help.

2. Most students will only succeed in an environment in which they feel safe and supported.

Task 2.1

Answers will vary.

Reflection 2.2

Answers will vary.

Reflection 2.3

1. A safe classroom environment would provide a focus on academics, collaboration between students, and the opportunity to take risks.

2. Every student struggles in mathematics. Incredibly gifted mathematics students sometimes have trouble documenting or explaining their thinking. A classroom in which all students learn from one another, take risks, and academically support one another will benefit all students.

3. Answers will vary.

4. Teachers must physically arrange the classroom so that they are able to access all groups and move freely throughout the classroom during student discussions to monitor for on-task math talk and supportive behaviors.

5. Safety in the classroom is a non-negotiable. A reasonable initial intervention is to note to the class that a particular safety is not being honored. A discussion using a two-column table—what does safety look like and what does it sound like?—is warranted. A private conversation with the student(s) not honoring the safety can be followed by the standard discipline procedures. Follow conversations with action, and intervene early.

6. *Non-negotiable* means that it cannot be negotiated or accepted; it is unconditional. By displaying and referring to the safety graphic organizer, teachers emphasize that these behaviors are non-negotiable.

Reflection 2.4

1. *Cooperative learning* is a set of structures for facilitating groups working together.

2. When students are working in cooperative groups toward a common goal, they have a sense of purpose and belonging.

3. Off-task behavior and inappropriate student interaction are two of the challenges when implementing cooperative learning.

Task 2.2

Answers will vary.

Reflection 2.5

A safe classroom environment will give Rafael the opportunity to learn from and engage safely with his peers. When struggling he will have the opportunity for immediate peer help. The safety graphic organizer will give a framework for his behavior in the classroom by emphasizing actions and words that help everyone succeed.

A safe classroom environment will give Andy the opportunity to learn from and engage safely with his peers. When struggling, he will have the opportunity for immediate peer help when stumped reading a question. The safety graphic organizer will give a framework for his behavior in the classroom by emphasizing 100 percent participation.

A safe classroom environment will allow Rachelle to take risks in class and work appropriately with other students when stumped. Peer tutors can ask appropriate facilitation questions to lead her to long-term mathematical understandings. The safety graphic organizer will give a framework for her behavior in the classroom by acknowledging that mistakes are OK (it's how we learn).

Organizing a safe classroom environment is critical when a student like Zack is part of the classroom. In order for learning to occur, students need to feel that their most basic needs will be taken care of. A safe classroom environment will give Zack a framework in which to guide his behavior. The opportunity for connecting with others is created. This classroom may be one of the few places where Zack feels safe. The safety graphic organizer provides a framework to guide the behavior of Zack and his classmates.

Reflection 3.1

Answers will vary.

Task 3.1

Answers will vary.

Task 3.2

Answers will vary.

Reflection 3.2

1. When effective questioning is used regularly, more students are empowered to think about and refine mathematical understandings, and more students develop the skills to help others think about and refine mathematical understanding.

2. The struggling students would be challenged to think and be given the subtle message that rigorous thinking is expected.

3. Follow-up questions are the ultimate tool in differentiated instruction.

4. Rafael will have the opportunity to clarify understandings with classmates because he enjoys working with peers. The likelihood that Rafael will remain on task is increased.

   Andy will most likely become more engaged because he seems to like the back-and-forth dialogue involved in questioning. He is also given the opportunity to refine understandings by becoming appropriately engaged with his classmates.

   Because Rachelle would be articulating her understandings, there is a greater likelihood that the mathematics would be stored in her long-term memory. She will also have the opportunity to refine her understandings and clarify misconceptions.

   The dynamics of the questioning process allows Zack a platform to demonstrate his ability in mathematics, appropriately giving him status along with the opportunity to connect appropriately to others in the classroom.

5. What example(s) of the mathematical concept can you find in your visual dictionary?

How would you apply the mathematical concept or process to a topic in your visual dictionary?

Which visual images help you to visualize or picture in your head the mathematical concept or process?

6. Does the title of the section give us any clues about the mathematics we are going to study?

   How do the diagrams or pictures give us clues about the mathematics we are going to study?

   How might this relate to your family or community?

   What do you think will happen next?

7. What happens when something repeats?

   Do the colors of the beads repeat? How do you know?

   What do you notice about the order of colored beads in the necklace?

8. How would you describe this mathematical concept or process in your own words?

   Why would this mathematical concept be helpful to your family or community?

   What do you find easiest about this mathematical concept or process?

   What do you find most difficult about this mathematical concept or process?

Task 3.3

Answers will vary.

Task 3.4

Answers will vary.

Reflection 3.3

Answers will vary.

Reflection 3.4

1. A good assessment should improve student learning first and foremost. If it does not accomplish that, it is wasted time. Good assessments provide evidence of student understanding and inform instruction for teachers. The results of assessment should

be timely and informative, giving students authentic feedback on misconceptions and understandings.

2. Performance assessments allow for differentiation of responses and evidence of mathematical understanding. They assess critical thinking and provide opportunities for the synthesis of ideas. Selected-response items enable students to guess, often assess lower-level skills, and do not promote critical thinking.

3. Scaffolding techniques could include the following. Read and explain the performance assessment rubric to the students. Provide examples of meeting the expectations of the rubric and examples of not meeting the expectations of the rubric. Create a sample to which students can refer when doing assignments. Provide specific feedback on student work, which assists students in meeting the expectations of the performance rubric. Use simpler language and pictures or diagrams, which might assist students in remembering the expectations of the performance rubric.

Reflection 4.1

1. *Accommodations* are practices and procedures of presentation, response, setting, and timing or scheduling that provide equitable access during instruction and assessment.

2. Wearing glasses, sitting near the teacher, and having extra time are common accommodations in the classroom.

Reflection 4.2

Answers will vary.

Task 4.1

Answers will vary.

Reflection 4.3

Answers will vary.

Reflection 4.4

1. Answers will vary.

2. Students with memory problems can be encouraged to make cue cards that they keep in their folders to use when problem solving and on tests. The students will eventually phase out the use of the cue cards when they feel able to retrieve the information without the cards. Word walls that define important concepts in mathematics, list the

problem-solving steps, the problem-solving strategies, and research-based questioning strategies for K–2 mathematics will help students with memory problems.

Reflection 4.5

1. Answers will vary.

2. Using the 5E instructional model with cooperative learning keeps students engaged. Students with attention difficulties will benefit from sitting near the teacher and in a place where distractions are minimized. Keeping the classroom neat and uncluttered, where materials are organized and neatly arranged on shelves, will help students with attention difficulties.

Reflection 4.6

1. Answers will vary.

2. Bridging from the real world to concrete manipulatives to the pictorial to the abstract helps students with abstract reasoning difficulties. Teaching the students to create graphic organizers and encouraging their use will benefit these students.

Reflection 4.7

1. Answers will vary.

2. Keeping an agenda on the board so students will know the day's structure will benefit students with organizational deficits. Minimizing clutter on student pages will also benefit students with organizational deficits.

Reflection 4.8

1. Answers will vary.

2. Using engaging problems that are a part of the child's experience will help a child with cognitive processing deficits. Other strategies include physically or concretely modeling the problem situation or concept. Then instruct the student to create a drawing of the physical or concrete model. Then, connect the drawing to a graphic organizer, mat, or table that organizes the information in the drawing. Finally, connect the organizer, mat, or table to the mathematical notation. Provide an organizer that supports this process. Encourage prediction and estimation.

Reflection 4.9

1. Answers will vary.

2. The use of transparent color overlays may be helpful to some students with visual perception problems. Using dark-colored fonts and graphics may also benefit students with visual perception problems.

Reflection 4.10

1. Answers will vary.

2. Speaking slowly and clearly and using visual representations will help students with auditory perception problems. A seat near the teacher may also help students with auditory processing deficits.

Reflection 4.11

1. Answers will vary.

2. Providing example problems that include detailed solutions serve as a guide to students with metacognitive deficits when they are solving similar problems. Using think-alouds will also benefits students with metacognitive deficits.

Reflection 4.12

1. Answers will vary.

2. Providing clear verbal and written directions will help students with autism spectrum disorders. Alternating between preferred activities (which may include independent work) and unpreferred activities (which may include cooperative learning) may also help students with autism spectrum disorders.

Task 5.1

Explain the Developmental Progression	Check the Type(s) of Discourse Used	Describe the Activity	Create Questions That Would Facilitate Sense-Making
How does this phase stimulate curiosity? *Equally dividing a representation of a pizza stimulates curiosity.* How does this phase activate prior knowledge? *Students are familiar with dividing something equally.* What questions might students raise? *How can we make sure each person gets an equal amount?* What accommodations could be included in this phase to make learning more accessible? *Dividing actual pizzas or large cookies would connect to real life.*	✓ Student–Student ✓ Student–Teacher ✓ Teacher–Student	*An engaging question is posed to students. Students conjecture and create answers to key questions.*	*How would the equal pieces change if the pizza were divided among more students?*

Reflection 5.1

The teacher could display four different fractions such as $\frac{3}{4}$, $\frac{2}{3}$, $\frac{1}{5}$, and $\frac{1}{6}$ in the room. The teacher then provides each student with a picture model of one of the fractions (or its equivalent) displayed in the room. Students match their picture card to the displayed fraction.

Task 5.2

Explain the Developmental Progression	Check the Type(s) of Discourse Used	Describe the Activity	Create Questions That Would Facilitate Sense-Making
What concepts does this phase explore? *Understanding the relationship between equivalent fractions* What vocabulary will students need? *Relationship, fractional part, set model, equivalent, numerator, denominator* What accommodations could be included in this phase to make learning more accessible? *Examples of different representations, posted vocabulary words to use in the discussion, and publishing of results will help.*	✓ Student–Student Student–Teacher Teacher–Student	*As a group, students explore a solution to the problem. Students publish their work on chart paper.*	*What is the relationship between equivalent fractions?* *How would you describe equivalent fractions?*

Reflection 5.2

Ask students to determine which quantities can evenly create halves, thirds, fourths, and so on.

Task 5.3

Explain the Developmental Progression	Check the Type(s) of Discourse Used	Describe the Activity	Create Questions That Would Facilitate Sense-Making
What connections are essential for the student to understand? *Equivalent fractions have the same value. Equivalent fractions can be created by multiplying or dividing by the fractional equivalent of 1.* What new vocabulary is introduced? *Equivalent, fractional, set model mat, relationship* What algorithms are connected to the concept? *Students must multiply by fractional representation of 1 or fraction form of 1.* What accommodations could be included in this phase to make learning more accessible? *Display the concrete, pictorial, and numerical representation of equivalent fractions on the same paper.*	Student–Student ✓ Student–Teacher ✓ Teacher–Student	*Through questioning strategies, important mathematical connections are made explicit in this phase.* *Vocabulary is introduced and refined.*	*How would you describe a fractional representation of 1?* *What does* equivalent value *mean?*

Task 5.4

Explain the Developmental Progression	Check the Type(s) of Discourse Used	Describe the Activity	Create Questions That Would Facilitate Sense-Making
How is the new concept applied or extended? *The concept of equivalent is extended to include several representations.*	Student–Student ✓ Student–Teacher ✓ Teacher–Student	*Students extend their understanding of equivalent by comparing and contrasting various representations.*	*How are the different forms of representing equivalent fractions alike? How are they different?*
How is the use of vocabulary encouraged? *Students use vocabulary during dialogue and while comparing fraction match cards. The teacher could check off the vocabulary he or she hears as he or she walks around the room.*			*How would you describe creating an equivalent fraction by using a form of 1?*
What understanding must the student have to be successful with this phase of the lesson? *Equivalent values can be represented several ways.*			
How (if at all) must the algorithms be applied? *Students must convert a fraction to an equivalent fraction.*			
What accommodations could be included in this phase to make learning more accessible? *Follow-up questions will refine understanding.*			

Reflection 5.3

Assign a fraction to each group. Ask groups to create as many equivalent representations as possible on a piece of chart paper.

Task 5.5

Explain the Developmental Progression	Check the Type(s) of Discourse Used	Describe the Activity	Create Questions That Would Facilitate Sense-Making
What concepts are addressed in this phase? *The concept of equivalent fraction is applied using concrete models.*	Student–Student ✓ Student–Teacher ✓ Teacher–Student	*Students individually solve a problem using the concept of equivalent fractions.*	*What do you know?* *What do you need to know?*
What additional skills must the students have to successfully complete this phase? *They must be able to read and understand the problem, and then explain the solution by using appropriate language and vocabulary skills.*		*Students are expected to explain their solution.*	*Which strategy would be useful in solving the problem?*
What accommodations could be included in this phase to make learning more accessible? *The student may be given the option of verbally explaining the solution strategy or dictating it to a peer tutor.*			*How could this problem be represented?* *How do you know your answer is reasonable?*

Reflection 5.4

1. Rafael could place his vocabulary organizer in his dictionary. He could draw pictures to show equivalent fractions.

2. The performance assessment could be read aloud to Andy.

3. The follow-up questions will help Rachelle refine her thinking. The questions will allow her to connect the various fraction models to the various symbolic equivalence.

4. Creating a poster allows Zack to draw pictures. This allows him to share his thinking with others.

Task E.1

Answers will vary.

Reflection E.1

1. The structured cooperative learning activities appeal to Rafael's preference for routine, scaffold the need for students with autism to refine their understanding of the purpose of communication, allow Rafael the opportunity to engage with classmates, stretch his language skills, and help him learn how to articulate his needs through the modeling his classmates provide.

2. The 5E lesson model gives Andy the opportunity for engaged, active learning. He is more likely to stay on task, and the dialogue and problem solving with classmates will improve his mathematical understandings and grades.

3. Multiple representations and the opportunity to dialogue and refine mathematical understandings will help to fill in the gaps in Rachelle's understandings and increase her retention of mathematics.

4. The safety graphic organizer will provide a safe environment for Zack and his classmates because the expectations are clearly defined and refined over the school year in a positive, instructive format.

Reflection E.2

Answers will vary.

Task E.2

Answers will vary.

Reproducibles for Lessons in Chapters 5 and 6

Set Model Mat: Halves

$$\frac{1}{2}$$

$$\frac{1}{2}$$

Set Model Mat: Thirds

$\frac{1}{3}$

$\frac{1}{3}$

$\frac{1}{3}$

Set Model Mat: Fourths

$$\frac{1}{4}$$

$$\frac{1}{4}$$

$$\frac{1}{4}$$

$$\frac{1}{4}$$

Set Model Mat: Sixths

$\frac{1}{6}$

$\frac{1}{6}$

$\frac{1}{6}$

$\frac{1}{6}$

$\frac{1}{6}$

$\frac{1}{6}$

Set Model Mat: Twelfths

$\dfrac{1}{12}$	$\dfrac{1}{12}$
$\dfrac{1}{12}$	$\dfrac{1}{12}$
$\dfrac{1}{12}$	$\dfrac{1}{12}$
$\dfrac{1}{12}$	$\dfrac{1}{12}$
$\dfrac{1}{12}$	$\dfrac{1}{12}$
$\dfrac{1}{12}$	$\dfrac{1}{12}$

Fraction Circles

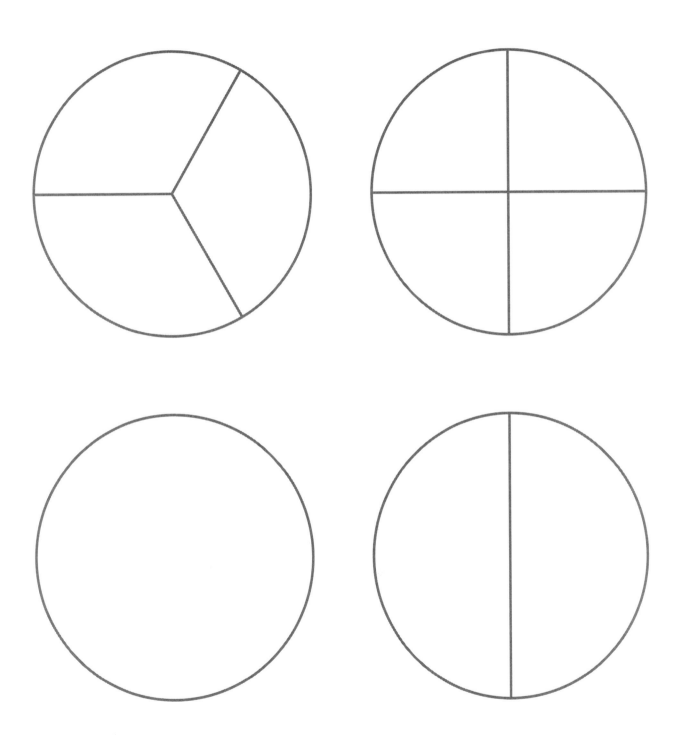

page 1 of 3

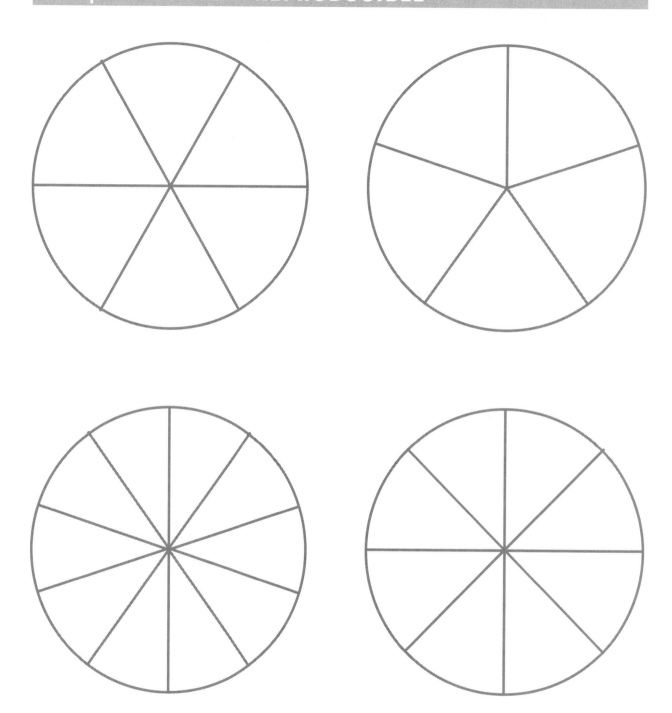

page 2 of 3

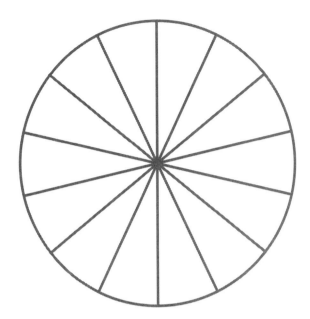

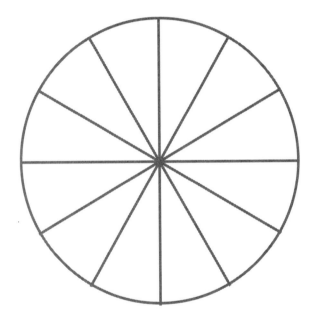

Making Math Accessible to Students With Special Needs (3–5) © 2010 r4 Educated Solutions • solution-tree.com
Visit **go.solution-tree.com/specialneeds** to download this page.

Multiplication Chart

x	1	2	3	4	5	6	7	8	9	10	11	12
1	1	2	3	4	5	6	7	8	9	10	11	12
2	2	4	6	8	10	12	14	16	18	20	22	24
3	3	6	9	12	15	18	21	24	27	30	33	36
4	4	8	12	16	20	24	28	32	36	40	44	48
5	5	10	15	20	25	30	35	40	45	50	55	60
6	6	12	18	24	30	36	42	48	54	60	66	72
7	7	14	21	28	35	42	49	56	63	70	77	84
8	8	16	24	32	40	48	56	64	72	80	88	96
9	9	18	27	36	45	54	63	72	81	90	99	108
10	10	20	30	40	50	60	70	80	90	100	110	120
11	11	22	33	44	55	66	77	88	99	110	121	132
12	12	24	36	48	60	72	84	96	108	120	132	144

Vocabulary Organizer: Equivalent Fractions

My Definition	Personal Association

Equivalent Fractions

Example	Nonexample

Fraction Match Cards

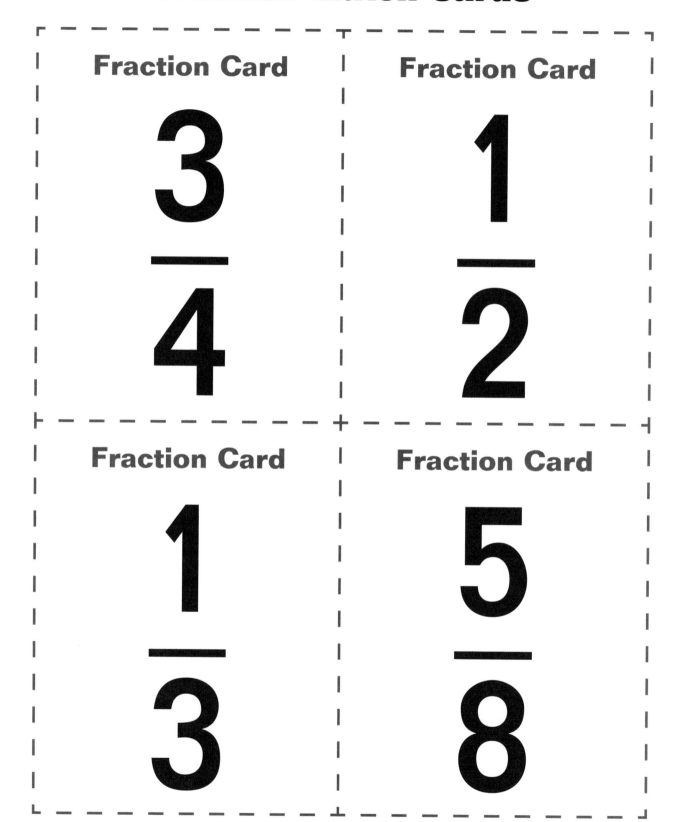

Fraction Card

$$\frac{3}{4}$$

Fraction Card

$$\frac{1}{2}$$

Fraction Card

$$\frac{1}{3}$$

Fraction Card

$$\frac{5}{8}$$

Making Math Accessible to Students With Special Needs (3–5) © 2010 r4 Educated Solutions • solution-tree.com
Visit **go.solution-tree.com/specialneeds** to download this page.

Area Model Card

Area Model Card

Area Model Card

Area Model Card

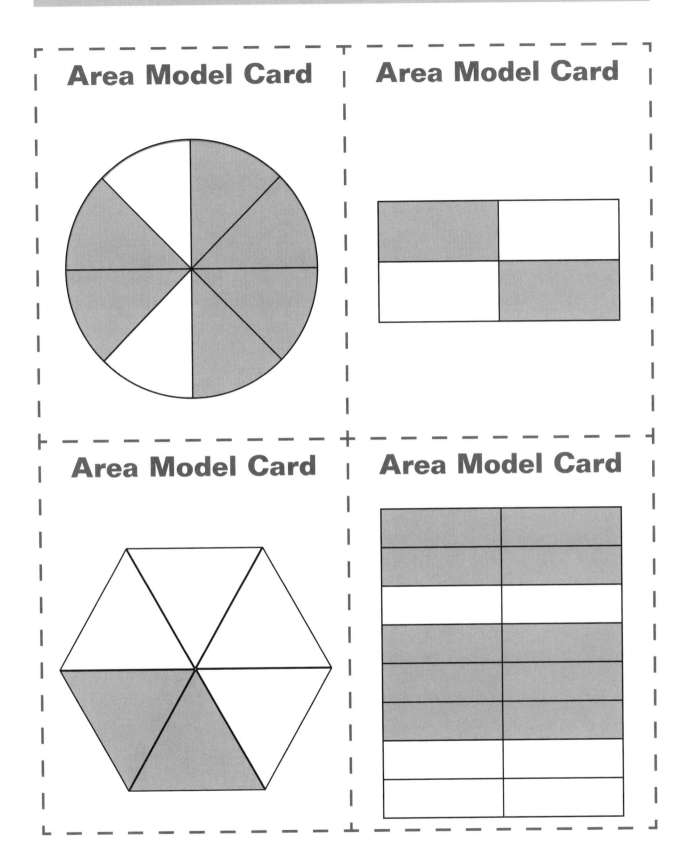

Set Model Card

Set Model Card

Set Model Card

Set Model Card

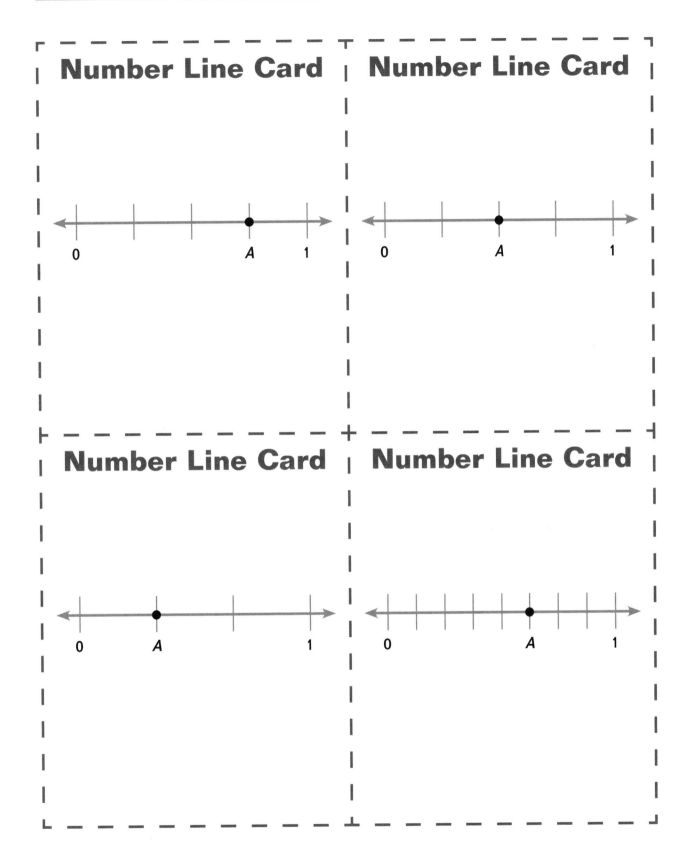

Number Line Card

Number Line Card

Number Line Card

Number Line Card

Performance Assessment

Use pattern blocks to create a fraction model of $\frac{1}{3}$. Create a model of a different fraction that is equivalent to $\frac{1}{3}$. Draw a picture of your models. Explain your thinking.

Each hexagon = 1

Garden Problem

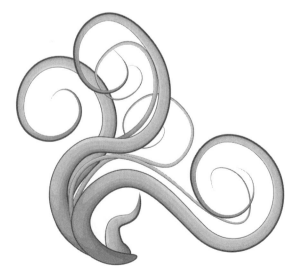

James is planting bean plants in his garden. He will plant 4 bean plants in each row. If there are 3 rows of bean plants in his garden, how many bean plants will James need?

Window Pane Problem-Solving Card

Station 1

Millie went on vacation for 4 weeks. If there are 7 days in one week, how many days was Millie on vacation?

Making Math Accessible to Students With Special Needs (3–5) © 2010 r4 Educated Solutions • solution-tree.com

Visit **go.solution-tree.com/specialneeds** to download this page.

Window Pane Problem-Solving Card

Station 2

Jim, Martin, and Clifton each purchased a set of 5 model cars. How many model cars did the 3 boys purchase in all?

Window Pane Problem-Solving Card

Station 3

Mrs. Milburn arranged the student desks in her classroom into 6 rows. There were 5 student desks in each row. How many student desks were in Mrs. Milburn's arrangement?

Window Pane Problem-Solving Card

Station 4

Judy has 3 fishbowls in her room. There are 11 fish in each fishbowl. How many fish does Judy have in her room in all?

Window Pane Problem-Solving Card

Station 5

Mr. Hakim placed math books in 4 stacks on a shelf. There were 9 math books in each stack. How many math books did Mr. Hakim place on the shelf?

Window Pane Problem-Solving Card

Station 6

Write your own problem using this story mat and Apple Counters.

Window Pane Problem-Solving Recording Sheet: Station 1

Use the calendar and counters to solve the problem.

Problem	Pictorial Representation
Millie went on vacation for 4 weeks. If there are 7 days in one week, how many days was Millie on vacation?	
Number Representation	**Explain Your Thinking**

Window Pane Problem-Solving Recording Sheet: Station 2

Use the beans and cups to solve the problem.

Problem	Pictorial Representation
Jim, Martin, and Clifton each purchased a set of 5 model cars. How many model cars did the 3 boys purchase in all?	
Number Representation	**Explain Your Thinking**

Window Pane Problem-Solving Recording Sheet: Station 3

Use the square tiles to solve the problem.

Problem	Pictorial Representation
Mrs. Milburn arranged the student desks in her classroom into 6 rows. There were 5 student desks in each row. How many student desks were in Mrs. Milburn's arrangement?	
Number Representation	**Explain Your Thinking**

Window Pane Problem-Solving Recording Sheet: Station 4

Use the counters and string loops to solve the problem.

Problem	Pictorial Representation
Judy has 3 fishbowls in her room. There are 11 fish in each bowl. How many fish does Judy have in all?	
Number Representation	**Explain Your Thinking**

Window Pane Problem-Solving Recording Sheet: Station 5

Use the unifix cubes to solve the problem.

Problem	Pictorial Representation
Mr. Hakim placed math books in 4 stacks on a shelf. There were 9 math books in each stack. How many math books did Mr. Hakim place on the shelf?	
Number Representation	**Explain Your Thinking**

Window Pane Problem-Solving Recording Sheet: Station 6

Write your own problem using the Station 6 story mat and Apple Counters.

Problem	Pictorial Representation
Number Representation	**Explain Your Thinking**

Calendar

Sunday	Monday	Tuesday	Wednesday	Thursday	Friday	Saturday

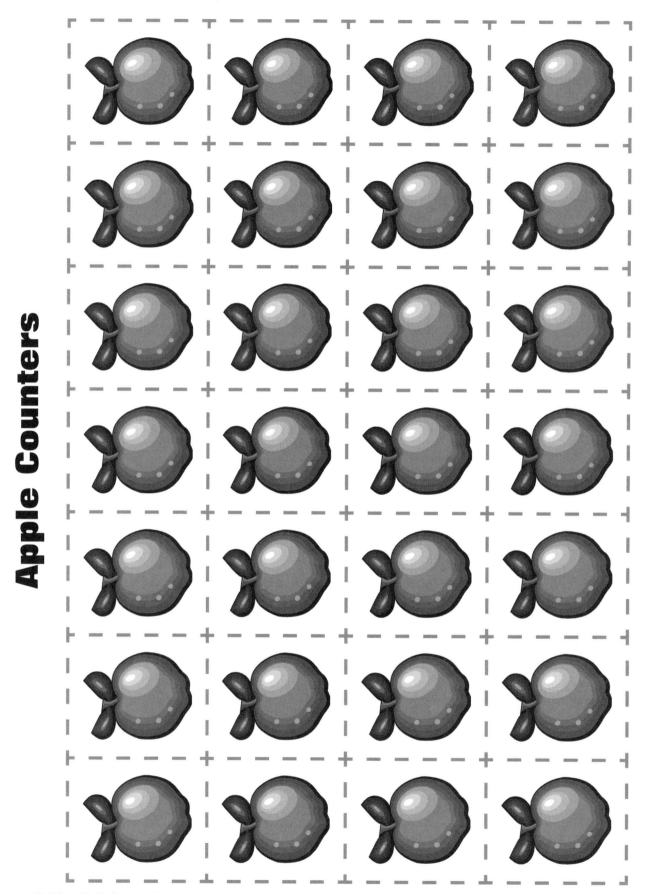

Apple Counters

Product Finders

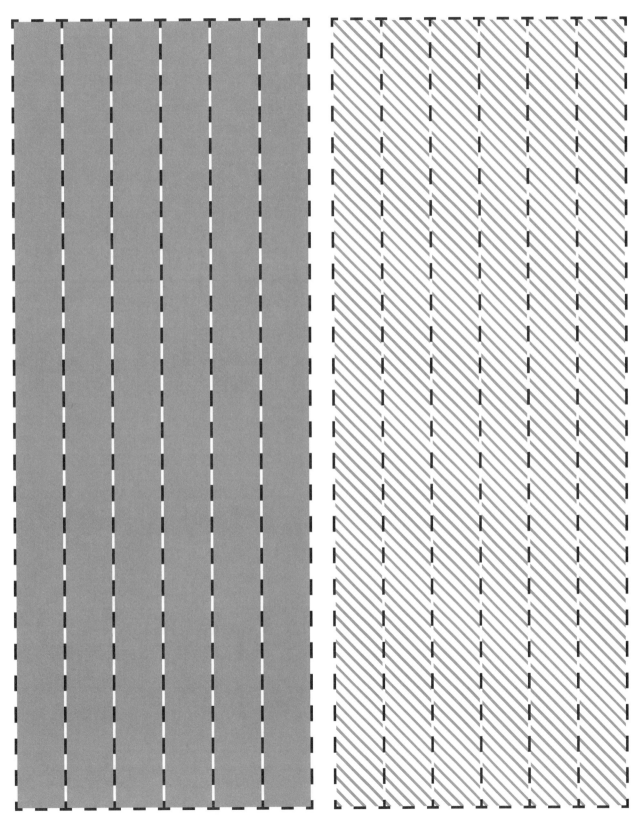

Vocabulary Organizer: Factor

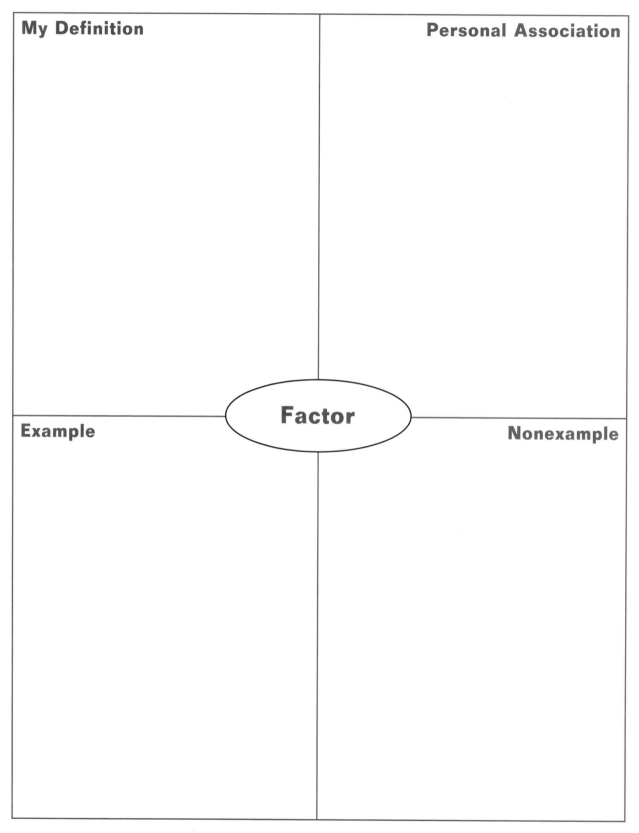

My Definition	Personal Association
Example	**Nonexample**

Factor

Vocabulary Organizer: Product

My Definition	Personal Association

Product

Example	Nonexample

The Product Is . . . 16

Use square tiles to build all of the possible arrays for the product listed. Draw the arrays on the grid. Record multiplication number sentences for each array. Write a story problem that can be solved using one of the number sentences.

All possible arrays:

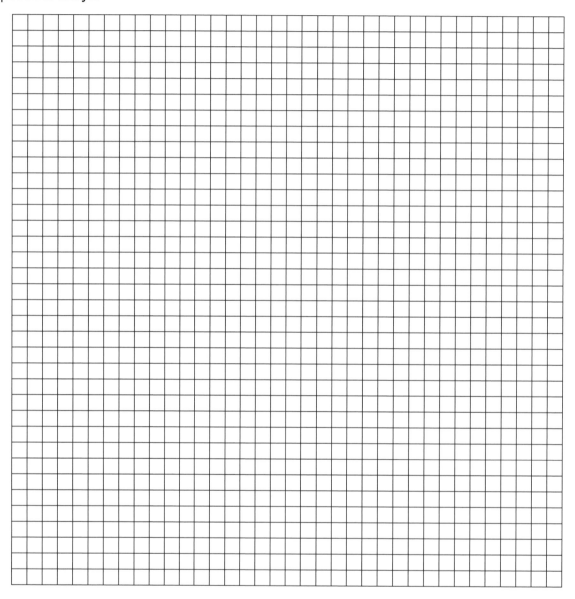

Number sentences:

Story problem:

The Product Is . . . 26

Use square tiles to build all of the possible arrays for the product listed. Draw the arrays on the grid. Record multiplication number sentences for each array. Write a story problem that can be solved using one of the number sentences.

All possible arrays:

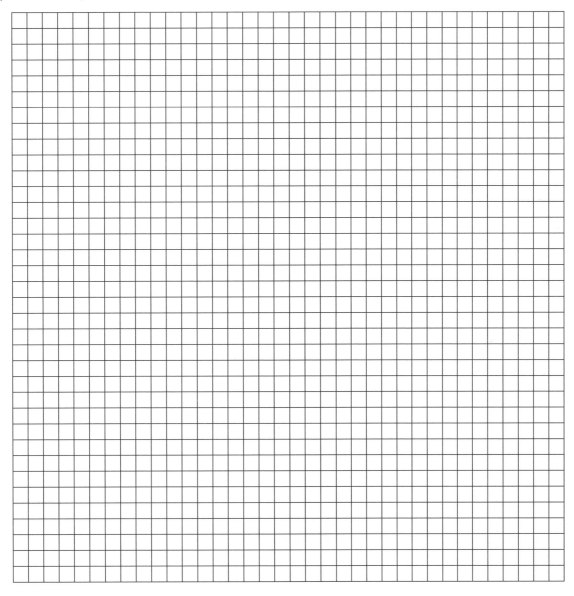

Number sentences:

Story problem:

The Product Is . . . 32

Use square tiles to build all of the possible arrays for the product listed. Draw the arrays on the grid. Record multiplication number sentences for each array. Write a story problem that can be solved using one of the number sentences.

All possible arrays:

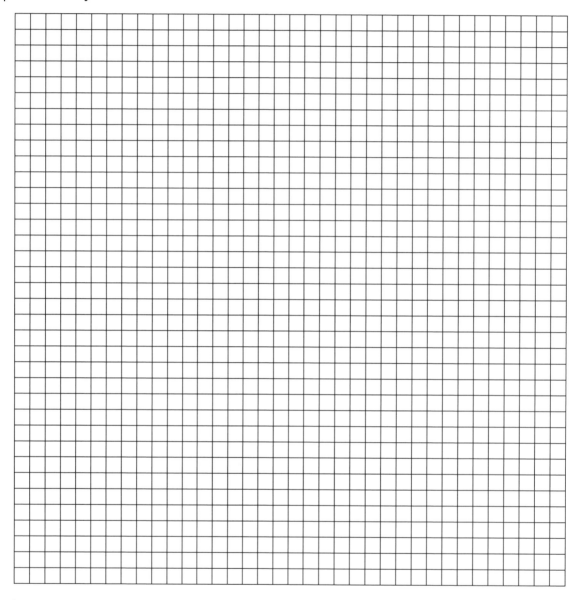

Number sentences:

Story problem:

The Product Is . . . 35

Use square tiles to build all of the possible arrays for the product listed. Draw the arrays on the grid. Record multiplication number sentences for each array. Write a story problem that can be solved using one of the number sentences.

All possible arrays:

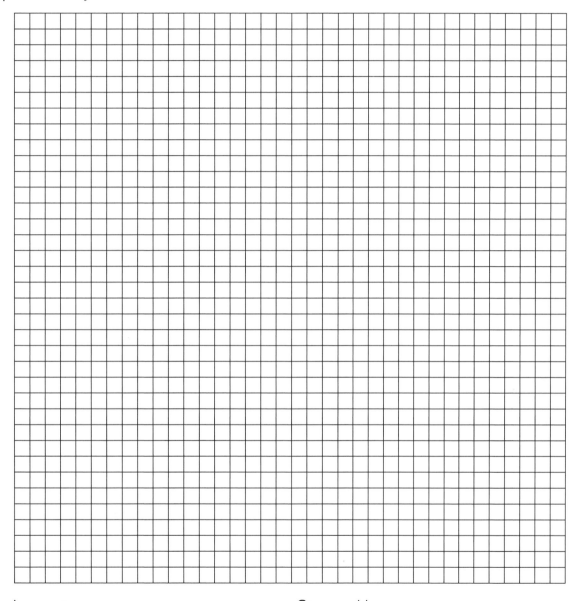

Number sentences:

Story problem:

Square-Inch Grid Paper

Square-Centimeter Grid Paper

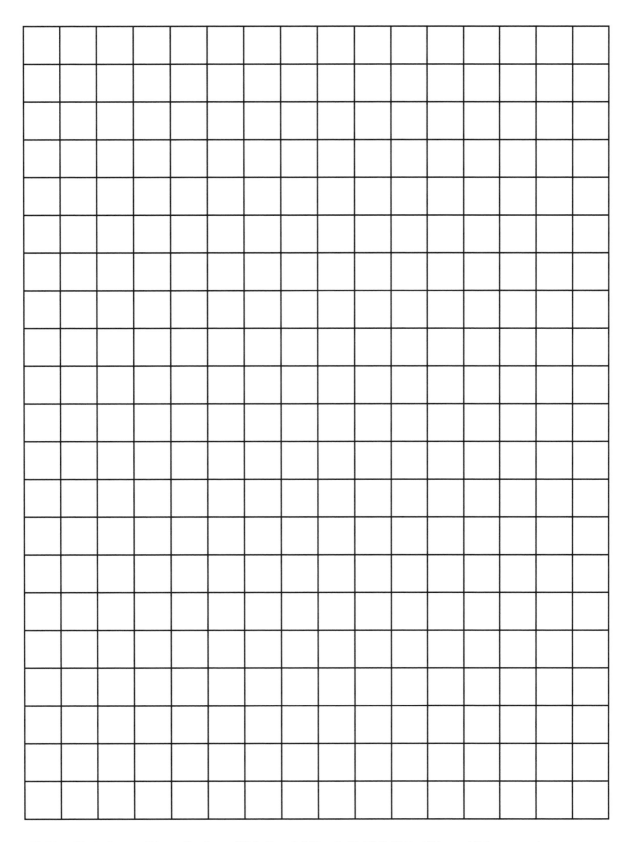

Performance Assessment

Use base-10 blocks to model the problem below. Draw your base-10 block model. Write a number sentence to represent the problem and solve it. Explain your thinking.

Each day, Larry delivers 23 newspapers to each block in his neighborhood. If his paper route is 7 blocks long, how many newspapers does Larry deliver each day?

Appendix C

Additional Resources

Questioning Sequence Checklist

Use this checklist to guide your reflections on the type of questioning used in your classroom or a peer's. (A peer coach can help by writing down questions during a ten-minute segment of instruction.) Write the questions in the left-hand column, then check the appropriate box to show what the question accomplishes in the classroom.

Question	Key Questions		Follow-Up Questions				
	Question Elicits One Answer	Question Elicits More Than One Answer	Question Clarifies Concepts or Terms	Teacher Verifies Student Response	Teacher Prompts Student to Refocus on Task at Hand	Teacher Allows Other Students to Respond to the Response	Teacher Guides the Student to Give a More Specific Answer

Student Rubric, Grades 3–5

I arrived at a correct solution. **Yes** **No**				
Criteria	**4**	**3**	**2**	**1**
Concept Understand the problem.	I understood how all of the parts of the problem fit together, so I could make sense of the problem.	I understood all of the parts of the problem, and I made partial sense of the problem.	I understood some of the parts of the problem.	I showed little to no understanding of the important facts of the problem that would help me find the answer.
Procedure Work the problem.	I used an appropriate strategy. I connected how I needed to do the problem with what I understood about the problem and my selected strategy. I did all of my math steps correctly.	I used an appropriate strategy. I connected how I needed to do the problem with what I understood about the problem and my selected strategy. I did some of my math steps correctly. I did not arrive at a correct solution because I made a careless mistake.	I used an appropriate strategy. I showed little connection between how I needed to do the problem and my selected strategy. I did some of my math steps correctly but reached an incorrect solution.	I used an inappropriate strategy. My work had lots of mistakes.
Communication Communicate what you understand. Communicate how you worked the problem.	I explained why I did what I did and supported my explanation with information from the problem. I used correct math vocabulary and notation.	I explained why I did what I did and supported my explanation with information from the problem. I used some correct math vocabulary and notation.	I gave little explanation of why I did what I did. I only explained what I did. I used some correct math vocabulary and notation.	I gave very little or no explanation of what I did. I used little or incorrect math vocabulary and/or notation.

Making Math Accessible to Students With Special Needs (3–5) © 2010 r4 Educated Solutions • solution-tree.com
Visit **go.solution-tree.com/specialneeds** to download this page.

Problem-Solving Organizer

Restate the problem using active voice and simple sentences. (Option: review with a partner and edit.)	
What do I know?	What do I need to know?
Which strategy would be useful in solving the problem? • Draw a picture or diagram • Look for a pattern • Guess and check • Act it out • Make a table • Work a simpler problem • Work backwards	How could this problem be represented? • Algebra tiles or manipulatives • Picture • Table • Diagram • Graph • Algebraically
Work the problem. Use the back if you need more space.	
Write the answer in a complete sentence:	Explain how you know your answer is reasonable:

Making Math Accessible to Students With Special Needs (3–5) © 2010 r4 Educated Solutions • solution-tree.com
Visit **go.solution-tree.com/specialneeds** to download this page.

Research-Based Questioning Strategies for 3–5 Mathematics

These metacognitive questions can help students at each stage of the problem-solving process. As students work with the Problem-Solving Organizer, remind them to ask themselves these questions.

Understand—See

- How can you say the problem using your own words?
- What more do you need to know?
- Could you draw a picture to show the problem?
- Have you solved a problem like this before?

Plan—Think

- Have you solved a problem like this before?
- What do you guess the answer might be?
- What plan will help you find an answer?
- What materials or tools do you need?
- How can you make this simpler?
- What kind of picture would help you?
- What patterns do you see that would help you?

> What am I doing?
>
> Why am I doing it?
>
> How is this helping me solve the problem?

Work—Do

- Is your plan working?
- How do you know?
- How could you explain what you did?
- How close to the answer was your guess?

Check

- Does your answer make sense?
- How could you solve this problem another way?
- Could you make another problem like this one?
- How close to the answer was your guess?

5E Lesson Plan Template

Learning Phase	Developmental Progression	Type of Discourse	Activity Description	Facilitation Questions
Engage	How does this phase stimulate curiosity? How does this phase activate prior knowledge? What questions might students raise? What accommodations could be included in this phase to make learning more accessible?	Student–Student Student–Teacher Teacher–Student		
Explore	What concept(s) will students explore? What new vocabulary will students need for this phase of the lesson? What accommodations could be included in this phase to make learning more accessible?	Student–Student Student–Teacher Teacher–Student		
Explain	What connections are essential for the student to understand? What new vocabulary is introduced in this phase? What algorithms (computational procedures) are connected to the concept? What accommodations could be included in this phase to make learning more accessible?	Student–Student Student–Teacher Teacher–Student		

Learning Phase	Developmental Progression	Type of Discourse	Activity Description	Facilitation Questions
Elaborate	How is the new concept applied or extended?	Student–Student Student–Teacher Teacher–Student		
	How will I encourage the use of vocabulary?			
	What concepts and processes must students understand to be successful with this phase of the lesson?			
	How (if at all) must the algorithms be applied?			
	What accommodations could be included in this phase to make learning more accessible?			
Evaluate	What concept(s) will I assess?	Student–Student Student–Teacher Teacher–Student		
	What additional skills must students have to complete this phase successfully?			
	What accommodations could be included in this phase to make learning more accessible?			

5E Lesson Plan Short Form

Use the 5E Lesson Plan Template to generate ideas for a high-quality mathematics lesson, then use the Short Form to describe activities and script facilitation questions.

	Standard:	
Engage	Activity:	
	Key Questions:	
	Follow-Up Questions:	Accommodations:
Explore	Activity:	
	Key Questions:	
	Follow-Up Questions:	Accommodations:
Explain	Activity:	
	Key Questions:	
	Follow-Up Questions:	Accommodations:
Elaborate	Activity:	
	Key Questions:	
	Follow-Up Questions:	Accommodations:
Evaluate	Activity:	
	Key Questions:	
	Follow-Up Questions:	Accommodations:

References and Resources

Aleven, V., Koedinger, K. R., & Cross, K. (1999). Tutoring answer-explanation fosters learning with understanding. In S. P. Lajoie & M. Vivet (Eds.), *Artificial intelligence in education, open learning environments: New computational technologies to support learning, exploration, and collaboration* [Proceedings of AIED-99] (pp. 199–206). Amsterdam: IOS Press.

American Psychiatric Association. (2000). *Diagnostic and statistical manual of mental disorders, text revision: DSM-IV-TR* (4th ed.). Washington, DC: Author.

Americans with Disabilities Act of 1990, Pub. L. No. 101–336, § 2, 104 Stat. 328 (1991). Accessed at www.ada.gov/pubs/ada.htm on October 12, 2009.

Anderman, E., & Maehr, M. (1994). Motivation and schooling in the middle grades. *Review of Educational Research, 64*(2), 287–309.

Anderson, L. W., & Krathwohl, D. R. (2001). *A taxonomy for learning, teaching, and assessing.* New York: Longman.

Atwood, V. A., & Wilen, W. W. (1991). Wait time and effective social studies instruction: What can research in science education tell us? *Social Education, 55,* 79–81.

Austin, J., Burkhardt, J., & Jacobs, J. (2004, July 14). *Lt. Governor's Commission on Higher Education & Economic Growth: Background briefing for commission members.* Accessed at www.cherrycommission.org/docs/Resources/Background%20Briefing%20-%20Austin.pdf on October 11, 2009.

Baker, E. L., O'Neill, H. F., Jr., & Linn, R. L. (1993). Policy and validity prospects for performance-based assessments. *American Psychologist, 48,* 1210–1218.

Ball, D. L., Ferrini-Mundy, J., Kilpatrick, J., Milgram, J., Schmid, W., & Schaar, R. (2005). Reaching for common ground in K–12 mathematics education. *Notices of the American Mathematical Society, 52*(9), 1055–1058.

Ball, D. L., Hill, H. C., & Bass, H. (2005). Knowing mathematics for teaching: Who knows mathematics well enough to teach third grade, and how can we decide? *American Educator, 29*(3), 14–17, 20–22, 43–46.

Bamburg, J. (1994). Raising expectations to improve student learning. *North Central Regional Educational Laboratory Urban Education Monograph Series*. Accessed at www.ncrel.org/sdrs/areas/issues/educatrs/leadrshp/le0bam.htm on November 22, 2009.

Bandura, A. (1994). Self-efficacy. In V. S. Ramachaudran (Ed.), *Encyclopedia of human behavior* (Vol. 4, pp. 71–81). San Diego, CA: Academic Press. (*Encyclopedia of mental health*, by H. Friedman, Ed., 1998, San Diego, CA: Academic Press)

Bell, N., & Tuley, K. (2003). Imagery: The sensory-cognitive connection for math. *LD Online*. Accessed at www.ldonline.org/article/5647 on October 30, 2009.

Beyer, B. K. (1997). *Improving student thinking*. Boston: Allyn & Bacon.

Boaler, J. (2006, Winter). Opening our ideas: How a detracked mathematics approach promoted respect, responsibility, and high achievement. *Theory Into Practice, 45*(1). Accessed at www.msri.org/calendar/attachments/workshops 388/Open_our _ideas_Boaler.pdf on May 16, 2006.

Bos, C. S., & Vaughn, S. (1994). *Strategies for teaching students with learning and behavioral problems* (3rd ed.). Boston: Allyn & Bacon.

Bradley, R., Danielson, L. C., & Hallahan, D. P. (Eds.). (2002). *Identification of learning disabilities: Research to practice*. Mahwah, NJ: Erlbaum.

Brennan, A. D., & Dunlap, W. P. (1985). What are the prime factors of reading mathematics? *Reading Improvement, 22*, 152–159.

Brook, J., Nomura, C., & Cohen, P. (1989). A network of influences on adolescent drug involvement: Neighborhood, school, peer, and family. *Genetic, Social, and General Psychology Monographs, 115*(1), 303–321.

Burris, C. C., Heubert, J. P., & Levin, H. M. (2004). Math acceleration for all. *Improving Achievement in Math and Science, 61*, 68–71.

Butterworth, B. (1999). *The mathematical brain*. New York: Macmillan.

California Department of Education. (1990). *Enhancing opportunities for higher education among underrepresented students*. Sacramento, CA: Author.

Carey, K. (2004). *A matter of degrees: Improving graduation rates at four-year colleges and universities*. Washington, DC: Education Trust.

Clark, B. (1992). *Growing up gifted*. New York: Macmillan.

Cohen, J. (1969). *Statistical power analysis for the behavioral sciences*. New York: Academic Press.

Corville-Smith, J., Ryan, B. A., Adams, G. R., & Dalicandro, T. (1998). Distinguishing absentee students from regular attenders: The combined influence of personal, family, and school factors. *Journal of Youth and Adolescence, 27*(5), 629–640.

Costa, A., & Lowery, L. (1989). *Techniques for teaching thinking*. Pacific Grove, CA: Midwest Publications.

Cotton, K., & Wikelund, K. R. (1989). Parent involvement in education. *School Improvement Research Series, Close-Up 6*. Accessed at www.nwrel.org/scpd/sirs/3/cu6.html on March 4, 2010.

Covey, S. R. (1989). *The seven habits of highly effective people: Restoring the character ethic*. New York: Fireside.

Culyer, R. C. (1988). Reading and mathematics go hand in hand. *Reading Improvement, 25*, 189–195.

Cushman, K. (2005). *Sent to the principal: Students talk about making high schools better.* Providence, RI: Next Generation.

Daniel R. R. v. State Board of Education, 874 F.2d1036 (5th Cir.). (New York Court of Appeals, 1989). Accessed at www.uwyo.edu/wind/edec5250/assignments/Daniel.pdf on October 12, 2009.

Dantonio, M. (1990). *How can we create thinkers? Questioning strategies that work for teachers.* Bloomington, IN: National Educational Service.

Dantonio, M., & Beisenherz, P. C. (2001). *Learning to question, questioning to learn: Developing effective teacher questioning practices.* Boston: Allyn & Bacon.

Davidson, N. (1989). Small-group cooperative learning in mathematics: A review of the research. In N. Davidson & R. Dees (Eds.), *Research in small-group cooperative learning in mathematics,* monograph of the *Journal for Research in Mathematics Education.*

Edmonds, R. (1986). Characteristics of effective schools. In U. Neisser (Ed.), *The school achievement of minority children: New perspectives* (pp. 93–104). Hillsdale, NJ: Lawrence Erlbaum.

Education for All Handicapped Children Act of 1975. Accessed at www.ed.gov/policy/speced/leg/idea/history.html on October 11, 2009.

Education Trust. (2004). The real value of teachers. *Thinking K–16, 8*(1). Accessed at www2.edtrust.org/NR/rdonlyres/5704CBA6-CE12-46D0-A852-D2E2B4638885/0/Spring04.pdf on October 10, 2009.

Elliott, S. N. (1994). *Creating meaningful performance assessments: Fundamental concepts.* Reston, VA: Council for Exceptional Children.

Erickson, H. L. (2002). *Concept-based curriculum and instruction.* Thousand Oaks: Corwin Press.

Fletcher, J. M., Lyon, G. R., Barnes, M., Stuebing, K. K., Francis, D. J., Olson, R. K., et al. (2002). Classification of learning disabilities: An evidence-based evaluation. In R. Bradley, L. Danielson, & D. P. Hallahan (Eds.), *Identification of learning disabilities: Research to practice* (pp. 185–250). Hillsdale, NJ: Erlbaum.

Frayer, D. A., Frederick, W. C., & Klausmeier, H. J. (1969). *A schema for testing the level of concept mastery* (Tech. Rep. No. 16). Madison: University of Wisconsin Research and Development Center for Cognitive Learning.

Freeman, B. J. (1997). Guidelines for evaluating intervention programs for children with autism. *Journal of Autism and Developmental Disorders, 27,* 641–650.

Friend, M., & Bursuck, W. D. (2002). *Including students with special needs: A practical guide for classroom teachers* (3rd ed.). Boston: Allyn & Bacon.

Gardner, H. (1993). *Multiple intelligences: The theory in practice.* New York: HarperCollins.

Gardner, H., & Hatch, T. (1989). Multiple intelligences go to school: Educational implications of the theory of multiple intelligences. *Educational Researcher, 18*(8), 4–9.

Gersten, R. (2002, February 6). *Math education and achievement.* Paper presented at the U.S. Department of Education working group conference on the use of scientifically based research, Washington, DC. Accessed at www.ed.gov/nclb/methods/whatworks/research/page_pg6.html on October 19, 2009.

Glass, G. V., McGaw, B., & Smith, M. L. (1981). *Meta-analysis in social research.* Beverly Hills, CA: Sage.

Goldstein, S., & Goldstein, M. (1998). *Managing attention-deficit hyperactivity disorder in children: A guide for practitioners* (2nd ed.). New York: Wiley.

Good, T. L., & Brophy, J. E. (1986). *Educational psychology* (3rd ed.). New York: Longman.

Heward, W. L. (2006). *Exceptional children: An introduction to special education* (8th ed.). Upper Saddle River, NJ: Pearson Education.

Howard, J. (1990). *Getting smart: The social construction of intelligence.* Lexington, MA: The Efficacy Institute.

Individuals with Disabilities Education Act, Amendments of 1997, 20U.S.C. § 1400 *et. seq.* Accessed at www.ed.gov/offices/OSERS/Policy/IDEA/regs.html on October 11, 2009.

Individuals with Disabilities Education Improvement Act of 2004, 20 U.S.C. § 1400 *et. seq.* Accessed at http://idea.ed.gov/ on October 11, 2009.

IES, National Center for Education Statistics. (n.d.). Trends in International Mathematics and Science Study (TIMSS). *Mathematics achievement of fourth- and eighth-graders in 2007.* Accessed at http://nces.ed.gov/timss/results07_math07.asp on October 11, 2009.

Jarvis, H. L., & Gathercole, S. E. (2003). Verbal and nonverbal working memory and achievements on national curriculum tests at 11 and 14 years of age. *Educational and Child Psychology, 20,* 123–140.

Jensen, E. (2005). *Teaching with the brain in mind* (2nd ed.). Alexandria, VA: Association for Supervision and Curriculum Development.

Johnson, D. W., & Johnson, R. (1989). *Cooperation and competition: Theory and research.* Edina, MN: Interaction Book Company.

Johnson, D., & Johnson, R. (1990). *Learning together and alone.* New York: Prentice Hall.

Kagan, S. L., & Hallmark, L. G. (2001). Early care and education policies in Sweden: Implications for the United States. *Phi Delta Kappan, 83*(3), 237–245.

Knapp, M. S., Shields, P. M., & Turnbull, B. J. (1992). *Academic challenges for the children of poverty.* Summary report. Washington, DC: U.S. Department of Education.

Kohn, A. (1993). Choices for children: Why and how to let students decide. *Phi Delta Kappan, 75*(1), 8–20.

Kujawa, S., & Huske, L. (1995). *The strategic teaching and reading project guidebook* (Rev. ed.). Oak Brook, IL: North Central Regional Educational Laboratory.

Lehr, F., Osborn, J., & Hiebert, E. H. (2005). *A focus on vocabulary.* Accessed at www.prel.org/products/re_/ES0419.htm on March 4, 2010.

Levin, H. (1988). Accelerated schools for disadvantaged students. *Educational Leadership, 44*(6), 19–21.

Light, J. G., & DeFries, J. C. (1995). Comorbidity of reading and mathematics disabilities: Genetic and environmental etiologies. *Journal of Learning Disabilities, 28*(2), 96–106.

Marzano, R. J. (2003). *What works in schools: Translating research into action.* Alexandria, VA: Association for Supervision and Curriculum Development.

Marzano, R. J., Gaddy, B. B., & Dean, C. (2000). *What works in classroom instruction.* Aurora, CO: Mid-continent Research for Education and Learning.

Mastropieri, M. A., & Scruggs, T. E. (1998). *Enhancing school success with mnemonic strategies.* Accessed at www.vcld.org/pages/newsletters/00_01_fall/mnemonic.htm on March 6, 2006.

Mehan, H., Hubbard, L., & Villanueva, I. (1994). Forming academic identities: Accommodation without assimilation among involuntary minorities. *Anthropology and Education Quarterly, 25*(2), 91–117.

National Association of Secondary School Principals. (2004). *Breaking ranks II: Strategies for leading high school reform.* Providence, RI: Education Alliance.

National Center for Education Statistics. (2009). NAEP Data Explorer. *Do you have questions about what the nation's students know and can do?* Accessed at http://nces.ed.gov/nationsreportcard/naepdata/ on March 4, 2010.

National Council of Teachers of Mathematics. (2000). *Principles and standards for school mathematics.* Reston, VA: Author.

National Council of Teachers of Mathematics. (2007). Effective strategies for teaching students with difficulties in mathematics. *Instruction Research Brief.* Accessed at www.nctm.org/news/content.aspx?id=8452 on October 11, 2009.

National Institute of Nursing Research and the National Institute of Mental Health. (2005). *Less sleep, more struggles for elementary and middle school students.* Accessed at www.brown.edu/Administration/News_Bureau2005–06/05–046.html on March 16, 2006.

National Research Council. (2000). *Inquiry and the national science education standards.* Washington, DC: National Academies Press.

No Child Left Behind Act of 2001, 20 U.S.C. § 6301 (2002). Accessed at www.ed.gov/policy/elsec/leg/esea02/index.html on October 11, 2009.

Oakes, J. (1985). *Keeping track: How schools structure inequality.* New Haven, CT: Yale University Press.

Ornstein, R., & Thompson, R. (1984). *The amazing brain.* Boston: Houghton Mifflin.

Perner, L. (2002, July 17–21). *Preparing to be nerdy where nerdy can be cool: College planning for the high functioning student with autism.* Paper presented at the 2002 annual meeting of the Autism Society of America. Accessed at www.aspennj.org/pdf/information/articles/college-planning-for-the-high-functioning-student-with-autism.pdf on October 19, 2009.

Pintrich, P., & Schrunk, D. (1996). *The role of expectancy and self-efficacy beliefs.* Accessed at www.des.emory.edu/mfp/PS.html on November 23, 2009.

Polya, G. (1957). *How to solve it* (2nd ed.). Princeton, NJ: Princeton University Press.

President's Commission on Excellence in Special Education. (2001). *A new era: Revitalizing special education for children and their families.* Accessed at www.ed.gov/inits/commissionsboards/whspecialeducation/reports.html on October 11, 2009.

Prichett, P. (2001). *Mindshift: The employee handbook for understanding the changing world of work.* Dallas, TX: Pritchett.

Readence, J. E., Bean, T. W., & Baldwin, R. S. (1989). *Content area reading: An integrated approach.* Dubuque, IA: Kendall/Hunt.

Rehabilitation Act of 1973, 29 U.S.C. § 794. Accessed at www.dotcr.ost.dot.gov/documents/ycr/REHABACT.HTM on October 12, 2009.

Reigle, R. P. (1976). Classifying classroom questions. *Journal of Teacher Education, 27,* 156–161.

Richards, J. C. (2006). *Cooperative learning and secondary language teaching.* New York: Cambridge University Press.

Riley, J. P. (1981). The effects of preservice teachers' cognitive questioning level and redirecting on student science achievement. *Journal of Research in Science Teaching, 18,* 303–309.

Rowe, M. B. (1972). *Wait-time and rewards as instructional variables, their influence in language, logic, and fate control.* Paper presented at the National Association for Research in Science Teaching, Chicago.

Rowe, M. B. (1987, Spring). Wait time: Slowing down may be a way of speeding up. *American Educator, 11,* 38–43, 47.

Rutter, M., Maughan, B., Mortimore, P., Ouston, J., & Smith, A. (1979). *Fifteen thousand hours.* Cambridge, MA: Harvard University.

Sapon-Shevin, M., & Schniedewind, N. (1993, March). Why (even) gifted children need cooperative learning. *Educational Leadership,* 62–63.

Schmoker, M. (2001). *The* Results *fieldbook.* Alexandria, VA: Association for Supervision and Curriculum Development.

Scholtes, P. R. (1988). *The team handbook: How to use teams to improve quality.* Madison, WI: Joiner.

Schumaker, J. S., & Lenz, L. (1999). *Adapting language arts, social studies, and science materials for the inclusive classroom.* Reston, VA: Council for Exceptional Children.

Scollon, R., & Scollon, S. W. (2001). *Intercultural communication: A discourse approach* (2nd ed.). Oxford, England: Blackwell.

Scruggs, T. E., & Mastropieri, M. A. (1994). The construction of scientific knowledge by students with mild disabilities. *Journal of Special Education, 28*(3), 307–321.

Serwach, J. (2005). (2006, January 9). Who understands math well enough to teach it to 3rd graders? *University of Michigan Record Online.* Accessed at www.ur.umich.edu/news/index.html?Releases/2005/Dec05/v121205a on October 17, 2009.

Slavin, R. (1990). *Cooperative learning: Theory, research, and practice.* Englewood Cliffs, NJ: Prentice Hall.

Slavin, R., Karweit, N., & Madden, N. (1989). *Effective programs for students at risk.* Boston: Allyn & Bacon.

Smith, H. (2005). District-wide reform. In R. Young (Senior Producer), *Making schools work* [Television Broadcast]. Accessed at www.pbs.org/makingschoolswork/dwr/ny/index.html on October 10, 2009.

Stanford News Service. (1994, April 13). *Accelerated schools: Building on success.* Accessed at http://news.stanford.edu/pr/94/940413Arc4342.html on October 10, 2009.

Stewart, D., & Sun, J. (2004). The importance of social support from adults and peers in family, school and community settings: How can we build resilience in primary school aged children? *Asia Pacific Journal of Public Health, 16,* 37–41.

Taylor, A. R., Breck, S. E., & Aljets, C. M. (2004). What Nathan teaches us about transitional thinking. *Teaching Children Mathematics, 11,* 138–142.

Thomas, D. A. (1988). Reading and reasoning skills for mathematics problem solvers. *Journal of Reading, 32,* 244–249.

Tobin, K. (1987). The role of wait time in higher cognitive level learning. *Review of Educational Research, 57*(1), 69–95.

Trowbridge, L., & Bybee, R. (1996). *Teaching secondary school science: Strategies for developing literacy.* Englewood, Cliffs, NJ: Merrill.

United States Census Bureau. (2000). *Michigan highlights from the Census 2000 demographic files.* Accessed at http://factfinder.census.gov/home/saff/main.html?_lang =en on October 9, 2009.

United States Department of Education. (n.d.). *Building the legacy: IDEA 2004.* Accessed at http://idea.ed.gov/explore/view/p/%2Croot%2Cstatute%2CI%2CB%2C614%2Cd %2C on October 12, 2009.

United States Department of Education. (1995). *Individuals with Disabilities Education Act (IDEA) data (table AA3).* Accessed at www.ed.gov/pubs/OSEP95AnlRpt/index.html on January 11, 2010.

United States Department of Education, Elementary and Secondary Education. (2006, May 12). *Raising achievement: Alternate assessments for students with disabilities.* Accessed at www.ed.gov/policy/elsec/guid/raising/alt-assess-long.html on October 10, 2009.

United States Department of Education, National Center for Education Statistics. (2009). *Digest of education statistics, 2008* (NCES 2009-020). Accessed at http:// nces.ed.gov/Pubsearch/pubsinfo.asp?pubid=2009020 on January 11, 2010.

University of Texas Center for Reading and Language Arts/Texas Education Agency. (2003). *Three-tier reading model: Reducing reading difficulties for kindergarten through third grade students.* Austin, TX: Author.

Van de Walle, J. A. (2001). *Elementary and middle school mathematics: Teaching developmentally* (4th ed.). New York: Longman.

Waddle, J. L., & Conway, K. D. (2005, March 12). School reform through a school/university partnership. *Current Issues in Education, 8*(8). Accessed at http://cie.ed.asu .edu/volume8/number8/ on January 11, 2010.

Weinstein, R., Soule, C., Collins, F., Cone, J., Mehlorn, M., & Stimmonacchi, K. (1991). Expectations and high school change: Teacher-researcher collaboration to prevent school failure. *American Journal of Community Psychology, 19,* 333–363.

Weiss, I., & Pasley, J. (2004). What is high-quality instruction? *Educational Leadership, 61*(5), 24–28.

Wheelock, A. (1992). *Crossing the tracks: How "untracking" can save America's schools.* New York: The New Press.

Wigfield, A., & Eccles, J. S. (2000). Expectancy-value theory of achievement motivation. *Contemporary Educational Psychology, 25,* 68–81. Accessed at www.rcgd.isr .umich.edu/garp/articles/eccles00o.pdf on November 23, 2009.

Wilen, W. W. (1991). *Questioning skills for teachers.* Washington, DC: National Education Association.

Williamson, M. (1992). *Return to love: Reflections on the principles of a course in miracles.* New York: HarperCollins.

Winn, W., & Snyder, D. (1996). Cognitive perspectives in psychology. In D. H. Jonassen (Ed.), *Handbook of research for educational communications and technology* (pp. 112–142). New York: Simon & Schuster/Macmillan.

Wittrock, M. (Ed.). (1977). *The human brain.* Englewood Cliffs, NJ: Prentice Hall.

Wright, C. J., & Nuthall, G. (1970). Relationships between teacher behaviors and pupil achievement in three experimental elementary science lessons. *American Educational Research Journal, 7*(4), 477–491.

Index

A

abstract reasoning difficulties, students with, 81–82
Accelerated Learning, 38–39
accommodation plans (Section 504), 15
accommodations, 65–66. *See also* adaptations
accountability standards
    in cooperative learning, 27–28
    in NCLB, 10–11
adaptations
    defined, 66
    key questions for implementation plans, 67
adapting textbook lessons. *See* textbook lesson adaptation
adequate yearly progress (AYP), 11
ADHD (attention-deficit hyperactivity disorder), 79
affective needs, 20
alternative assessments, allowed in NCLB, 11
alternative placements, continuum of, 14
Alvarado, Anthony, 33
Anderson and Krathwohl's taxonomy, 42
ASD (autism spectrum disorders), 90–92
Asperger's syndrome, 90
assessments. *See* performance assessments
attention-deficit hyperactivity disorder (ADHD), 79
attention deficits, students with, 79–80
auditory discrimination learning disability, 16, 88
auditory processing deficits, 88–89

authentic assessments. *See* performance assessments
autism, 90
autism spectrum disorders (ASD), 90–92
AYP (adequate yearly progress), 11

B

Beisenherz, P. C., 41
Butterworth, David, 84

C

case studies
    description of, 16–17
    evaluating instructional strategies, 139
    facilitative questioning, 52
    graphic organizers, 60
    supportive classroom environment, 32
classroom atmosphere. *See* supportive classroom environment
cognitive processing deficits, 84–86
color-coding, 86
Concept Organizer (type of graphic organizer), 54
concepts, defined, 38
conceptual frameworks in mathematical instruction, 36
cooperative learning, 26–31
Covering the Bases team-building exercise, 26
cue cards, 78

D

Dantonio, M., 41
diagnostic strategic instruction in pyramid of student needs, 68–69
disability categories for students with special needs, 12
discrepancy model, 3
disruptive behavior, responding to, 49–50

E

Education for All Handicapped Children Act of 1975, 4
Einstein, Albert, 48, 65, 99
Elaborate (5E instructional model), 6, 97
    Fractional Parts sample lesson plan, 111–114
    textbook lesson adaptation, 132–133
emotional safety, 24
Engage (5E instructional model), 6, 96
    Fractional Parts sample lesson plan, 100–102
    textbook lesson adaptation, 124–127
Evaluate (5E instructional model), 7, 97. *See also* performance assessments
    Fractional Parts sample lesson plan, 114–115
    textbook lesson adaptation, 133–134
Explain (5E instructional model), 6, 97
    Fractional Parts sample lesson plan, 104–111
    textbook lesson adaptation, 130–132
Explore (5E instructional model), 6, 96–97
    Fractional Parts sample lesson plan, 103–104
    textbook lesson adaptation, 128–130

F

face-to-face interaction (in cooperative learning), 27–28
facilitative questioning, 41–52
    case studies, 52
    creating questioning sequences, 43–47
    responding to disruptive behavior, 49–50
    teaching questioning process, 43
    for vocabulary organizers, 56
    wait time for responses, 47–48
figure-ground processing difficulties, 86, 88
5E instructional model
    components of, 6–7, 95–97
        Fractional Parts sample lesson plan, 99–115
        Elaborate phase, 111–114

Engage phase, 100–102
Evaluate phase, 114–115
Explain phase, 104–111
Explore phase, 103–104
reproducibles for, 156–183
    lesson plan template, 98, 202–203
    multiple intelligences and, 99
    short form, 204
    textbook lesson adaptation, 124–134
        Elaborate phase, 132–133
        Engage phase, 124–127
        Evaluate phase, 133–134
        Explain phase, 130–132
        Explore phase, 128–130
        reproducibles for, 184–195
        steps in, 123–124
focused classroom environment, establishing, 23–26
follow-up questions, creating, 44–47
foundational instructional strategies, 69–75
    multiple intelligences and, 70
    multiple representations of concepts, 70–72
    prior knowledge, 70
    problem-solving strategies, 72–75
    tiered instruction, 75
Four Corners activity (cooperative learning), 31
Fractional Parts sample lesson plan, 99–115
    Elaborate phase, 111–114
    Engage phase, 100–102
    Evaluate phase, 114–115
    Explain phase, 104–111
    Explore phase, 103–104
    reproducibles for, 156–183
Frames of Mind (Gardner), 70

G

Gallery Walk activity (cooperative learning), 31
Gardner, Howard, 70
goals for cooperative learning strategies, 27–28
grades. *See* performance assessments
graphic organizers
    case studies, 60
    classroom safety example, 24
    developing understanding with, 52–60
    problem-solving organizers, 73–74, 200
    for students with organizational deficits, 83

H

heterogeneous grouping for team-building, 25–26

high expectations, importance of, 20–23

high-functioning individuals with autism (HFIWA), 91

high-quality instruction. *See also* supportive classroom environment
    developing understanding with graphic organizer, 52–60
    facilitative questioning, 41–52
        case studies, 52
        creating questioning sequences, 43–47
        responding to disruptive behavior, 49–50
        teaching questioning process, 43
        wait time for responses, 47–48
    implementation plan, 140–141
    importance of, 33–34
    indicators of, 58
    myths versus reality, 34–37
    performance assessments, 60–62
    in pyramid of student needs, 68–69
    teaching significant and appropriate content, 37–41

homework assignments in high-quality instruction, 40–41

How to Solve It (Polya), 72

I

IDEA 1997 (Individuals with Disabilities in Education Act of 1997), 3

IDEA 2004 (Individuals with Disabilities in Education Act of 2004), 2–4, 13–14

IEP (individualized education program), 65

incidental benefits, defined, 66

inclusion, 14–15

individual and group accountability (in cooperative learning), 27–28

individualized education program (IEP), 65

Individuals with Disabilities in Education Act of 1997 (IDEA 1997), 3

Individuals with Disabilities in Education Act of 2004 (IDEA 2004), 2–4, 13–14

instructional strategies
    case studies, 139
    evaluating, 137–138
    foundational instructional strategies, 69–75
    supplemental instructional strategies, 76–93

intellectual safety, 24

intelligences. *See* multiple intelligences

Interview the Expert activity (cooperative learning), 30

J

jigsaw activity (cooperative learning), 29

K

key questions
    for adaptation implementation plans, 67
    creating, 44–47

knowing mathematics, teaching mathematics versus, 35

L

language of mathematics, teaching, 40

learned helplessness, 77

least restrictive environment, 13–14

lesson planning. *See* 5E instructional model

Levin, Henry, 38

List-Group-Label (type of graphic organizer), 54

long-term memory, 76

Loud and Clear activity (cooperative learning), 30

M

Madwed, Sidney, 20

manipulatives, examples of, 71

The Mathematical Brain (Butterworth), 84

mathematics
    fundamental premises for teaching, 2
    importance of, 11–12
    language of, 40

Mathematics Performance Assessment Rubric, 61–62

McCarthy, Eugene, 19

memory deficits, students with, 76–79

metacognition, 40, 89

metacognitive deficits, students with, 89–90

mnemonic devices, songs as, 78

modifications, 65. *See also* adaptations

multiple intelligences
    5E instructional model and, 99
    teaching to, 70

multiple representations of concepts in foundational instructional strategies, 70–72

N

National Assessment of Educational Progress (NAEP), 10
National Council of Teachers of Mathematics, 65, 95
Newton, Isaac, 95
No Child Left Behind Act of 2001 (NCLB), 2, 10–11
nondiscrimination, 14–15
numerosity, 84

O

organizational deficits, students with, 82–84
organizational representations, 71–72

P

PDD-NOS (pervasive developmental disorder not otherwise specified), 90
PDD (pervasive developmental disorder), 91
performance assessments. *See also* Evaluate (5E instructional model)
    alternative assessments allowed in NCLB, 11
    in high-quality instruction, 60–62
pervasive developmental disorder not otherwise specified (PDD-NOS), 90
pervasive developmental disorder (PDD), 91
physical safety, 24
Polya, George, 72
positive interdependence (in cooperative learning), 27
President's Commission on Excellence in Special Education (2001), 2
prior knowledge
    in conceptual frameworks, 36
    in foundational instructional strategies, 70
    in key questions, 44
problem-solving cycle (RTI), 5
problem-solving organizers, 73–74, 200
problem-solving strategies, teaching, 72–75
processes, defined, 38
processing difficulties, students with, 84–89
pyramid of student needs, 68–69

Q

questioning process. *See also* facilitative questioning

research-based questioning strategies
    reproducible, 201
    teaching, 43
questioning sequences
    creating, 43–47
    reproducible for, 198

R

reflection questions, examples of, 44
Rehabilitation Act of 1973, Section 504, 14–15
remedial programs, effect of, 38
reproducibles
    5E instructional model short form, 204
    for Fractional Parts sample lesson plan, 156–183
    problem-solving organizers, 200
    questioning sequence checklist, 198
    research-based questioning strategies, 201
    student rubric, 199
    for textbook lesson adaptation, 184–195
requirements, mathematics instruction, 13–15
research-based instruction, 13. *See also* high-quality instruction
research-based questioning strategies
    reproducible, 201
response time (facilitative questioning), 47–48
response to intervention (RTI), 3–5
    principles of, 4–5
    problem-solving cycle, 5
reversals in reading, 86
rote learning, 34
Roundtable activity (cooperative learning), 30
RTI. *See* response to intervention (RTI)
rubrics, student rubric reproducible, 199. *See also* performance assessments

S

safe classroom environment, establishing, 23–26
Section 504 of Rehabilitation Act of 1973, 14–15
Semantic Feature Analysis (type of graphic organizer), 55
sequential memory, 76
short-term memory, 76
skills, defined, 38
sleep, lack of, 79
social safety, 24
songs, as mnemonic devices, 78

spatial organization difficulties, 88
spatial orientation difficulties, 86
special-needs students. *See* students with special needs
story mats, 70
strategies
    to convey high expectations, 22–23
    for cooperative learning, 27–28
    impact on student achievement, 53
student achievement, impact of strategies on, 53
student-centered classrooms, 20
student needs pyramid, 68–69
student rubric reproducible, 199
Student VOC (type of graphic organizer), 55
students with special needs
    disability categories for, 12
    mathematics instruction requirements, 13–15
    remedial programs, effect of, 38
    supplemental instructional strategies, 76–93
supplemental instructional strategies, 76–93
    abstract reasoning difficulties, students with, 81–82
    attention deficits, students with, 79–80
    autism spectrum disorders, students with, 90–92
    memory deficits, students with, 76–79
    metacognitive deficits, students with, 89–90
    organizational deficits, students with, 82–84
    processing difficulties, students with, 84–89
supportive classroom environment, 19–20. *See also* high-quality instruction
    case studies, 32
    cooperative learning in, 26–31
    high expectations, importance of, 20–23
    as safe and focused environment, 23–26

T

targeted intensive instruction in pyramid of student needs, 68–69

teaching mathematics, knowing mathematics versus, 35
team-building exercises, 25–26
Team-Pair-Solo activity (cooperative learning), 29–30
template for 5E instructional model, 98, 202–203
textbook lesson adaptation, 117–134
    Elaborate phase, 132–133
    Engage phase, 124–127
    Evaluate phase, 133–134
    Explain phase, 130–132
    Explore phase, 128–130
    reproducibles for, 184–195
    steps in, 123–124
think-alouds, 73
Think-Pair-Share activity (cooperative learning), 29
Three-Minute Review activity (cooperative learning), 29
tiered instruction, 75
time for responses (facilitative questioning), 47–48
traditional assessments, advantages/disadvantages, 60

V

Verbal and Visual Word Association (type of graphic organizer), 57
visual discrimination difficulties, 86
visual processing deficits, 86–88
Vocabulary Organizer (type of graphic organizer), 55–56

W

wait time for responses (facilitative questioning), 47–48
Williamson, Marianne, 9
window cut-outs, 88
working memory, 76

Solution Tree | Press

a division of

Solution Tree

Solution Tree's mission is to advance the work of our authors. By working with the best researchers and educators worldwide, we strive to be the premier provider of innovative publishing, in-demand events, and inspired professional development designed to transform education to ensure that all students learn.

r4 Educated Solutions

The core purpose of Region 4 is revolutionizing education to inspire and advance future generations.™ Instructional materials such as this publication are written and reviewed by content-area specialists who have an array of experience in providing quality, effective classroom instruction that provides the most impact on student achievement.